Autumn Exploration:

Uncovering the Treasures of Autumn

Published by Sophie Kilic
© Sophie Kilic 2025
The rights of Sophie Kilic to be identified as the
author of this work have been asserted by her
in accordance with the Copyright, Designs and
Patents Act of 1988.

ISBN 978-1-78792-096-5

Book design, layout and production management
by Into Print
www.intoprint.net
+44 (0)1604 832149

For my wonderful parents who have both inspired me through life. Thank you so much for everything you have done.

Contents

SEA SKETCHES

OUT AND ABOUT IN AUTUMN

WOOODLAND WONDERS

NIGHT LIFE

Introduction

The wind is picking up as I turn a new leaf and begin writing; a section of writing which will soon take shape and spread across this blank page. A dog barks once; a short sound enriching the stillness, enhancing the whisper of wind, an acorn's soft thud as it hits the soil, the phantom flick of leaves let loose, spiralling downwards to the ground, skittering on silent pathways. Each time the wind stirs, another one falls free, another is let loose. Yet the oak trees still hold many green leaves, clinging onto trapped sunlight in their sweet stores, savouring summer. Today has been warm and calm. Sunshine swept across the open spaces like liquid honey gilding leaves and causing berries to blaze in the hedgerows. But now the cloud has come, and the day is drawing to dusk, eking out the last dregs of daylight. In the pensive stillness only the branches of the oaks seem to slightly gesticulate, and with a crackle, another acorn falls, leaves floating like phantoms to the ground, the day done.

Autumn is a synthesis of seasons, a bridge between them with one side taking a nostalgic look back over the shoulder to summer as the kids kick their beachballs into a corner, flick off their flip flops or shake the sand from their shoes, ready to head back to begin the autumn term at school. The beach becomes less boisterous, emptied of holiday makers, dogs returning to race around the sand. Ice-cream kiosks close one by one, even if the weather is still like summer. Yet by the end of the season, after the clocks have changed, Christmas lights are already twinkling in trees and around windows, the Christmas market has been assembled with its alpine outdoor bar and skating rink and the days are drawing in. Yet autumn does stand alone in its own right. That brief burst of colour starting sometime mid- October and lasting barely three weeks before the storms roll in, wind ripping the last leaves from the trees.

Beginning meteorologically on September 1st and lasting until December 1st, autumn traditionally doesn't end until December 21st. This book will therefore be fairly flexible with what constitutes autumn's boundaries, preferring to follow the non-meteorological calendar. Autumn is traditionally a time for being industrious, for gathering in supplies before the hard winter bites. And yet it is a time of antic-ipation, full of flavour and hope, a time to be grateful for what we have. It provides a feast for all the senses, its tapestry of colours, textures, tastes and aromas all beautifully woven together. When one looks at the tangle of hedgerow studded with delicately structured ivy flowers, festooned with old man's beard, draped with the beads of black bryony and bejewelled with berries, one sees an example of this. Forests flood with colours on sunlit days when low sunshine streaks the forest floor and Illuminates food for foraging; the forms of fallen leaves, palmate, crinkled, oval, the open empty shells of horse chestnuts and the glint of conkers, the spiky discarded sweet chestnut cases sinking into soft soil. The earth exudes sweetness with the boozy ferment of fallen fruit and the richness of rotting leaves and cheeks colour like ripe apples in the cold.

Autumn is collectivist; it is a time for finding and keeping treasure to share and experience, a gathering in of resources, a strengthening of bonds. It is an exciting time of transition and change, but it is also a time of loss. These are tangible themes running through the veins of this book, themes which hopefully help us to savour the season which is to be treasured before we hunker down to winter.

HOMES AND GARDENS HOME

Beginnings

I will start my exploration of autumn at my childhood home. September was a time I always associated with the end of school summer holidays; trainers casually kicked off, leaving wistful wisps of sand across the terracotta tiled porch floor; the boat bag smelling of seaweed and salt, abandoned along with buckets, spades, shrimping nets and other beach paraphernalia; an odd flip flop cast away by the back door without its significant other. Outside on the drive the windsurfer waited to be stowed away. All of these things would be tidied up another time, later in the day, there was never any rush, our house being comfortably chaotic. Wet towels would be washed along with all the other beach gear, the trainers put with the wellington boots which were stored in a shabby, cobwebbed capacious wooden outhouse which was used for guinea pig hutches, apple storage and various outdoor activities plus all the clobber which went with them.

As a child still at school, the end of summer was always a time of unwanted change, even though we would go back to the beach throughout the autumn and winter (living as we did on the south coast just 5 miles from the beach as the crow flies). Despite being reunited with school friends, it was a time when butterflies flitted in stomachs at the onset of the new academic year; the dread of the unknown competing with the known apprehensions of early mornings, school runs and routines returning after a long and lazy summer holiday of late starts and spontaneity, fun with friends and family and carefree days on the beach. My brother would be back at boarding school and the house would seem to stand still and silently empty after he had gone, then there was the fact that the clocks would change, the days shorten, the nights lengthen, the leaves would fall from the trees. All these small changes seemed challenging and yet as I got older, change at this time of year took on a dimension of excitement: starting life at university, embarking on a new academic year of teaching abroad. Human beings do not naturally embrace change when it comes along, especially if it poses a threat or a challenge, but we often easily adapt or learn to face fears. Autumn is this time...

Still school age and living at home I

stared into the dingy and remote recesses of the outhouse, my wellies and walking boots waiting in cobwebbed corners. Soon they would be getting their airing, autumn adventures wading through woodland leaves and squelching through mud. My seaside trainers would also change colour on cross country runs. These were things to look forward to so that despite school and all the things we had to do, I eagerly anticipated autumn, its rich colours, comforting smells of wood, smoke and soil and its winding down to winter. The autumn term was one of the hardest regarding study, and later teaching in strange cities while hankering after home and the security of the countryside, yet autumn held many distractions outside the classroom to bring about a close connection with the real world, a beautiful winding down and the start of a creative cycle. I have continued to find this to be the case throughout my life.

Echoes of earlier autumns

It was one October that we moved house. My memories are fairly hazy for I was only eight, gripped by a sense of excitement that our house had three floors with a spiral staircase (up which the guinea pigs would hop) leading to an attic where my father ran a railway track around one of the rooms and through the loft. On the ground floor there was a music room where my mother taught clarinet, where she and my father would play chamber music with friends into the seemingly early hours and where my brother and I would reluctantly practice our instruments after school and with a little more enthusiasm, play family music at Christmas. The house had an expansive entrance hall; a square which served as a dining room at Christmas, and provided the central location for the grandfather clock, the heartbeat of the house.

There had been another grandfather clock in its place before us. When we had come to view the house, it had caught my eye because my favourite children's book, *Tom's Midnight Garden* had been centred around such a clock. What was more, the old lady who lived in the house and was selling it to us was a real Victorian and being in her presence was like entering a time-warp. On the day we moved in, we found her partaking of a leisurely breakfast set out on a silver tray, delicately imbibing tea (tea she insisted on being made from water boiled from the water-butt) while her butler and the removal men bustled around her. I found her fascinating, for

Tom's Midnight Garden had charmed me with the Victorian age and had produced in me a growing obsession. But then I had always loved anything old, from a fascination with fossils and dinosaurs cultivated at primary school, to an obsession with copying epitaphs in an old exercise book every time I went into a cemetery or church, and a love of stately homes. What a weird and curious child I must have been, but the old lady took a delight in me and gave me a book which she inscribed in wavering script. Kate Greenaway's *Language of Flowers* still takes pride of place in my bookcase. It is a book which I treasure from that time.

The house was not only situated next to a cemetery, which was great for collecting epitaphs, and also for visiting at night with my brother and spooking ourselves silly, but it also had a small secret shrubbery. The "shrubbery", which was really a woodland path wandering wild through the most secret part of the garden, was utterly idyllic and overgrown and I remember when my brother and I ventured into it on the first day we became hopelessly lost, clambering through the pittosporum and azaleas into the garden next door where the elderly neighbour, leaning on his wheelbarrow, kindly brought us back home. Once I had learned my way around and was no longer afraid of losing myself, I used to spend hours sitting in the "shrubbery", entirely secluded within walls of rhododendron, azalea and a shrub which I called the iced gem plant (*Kalmia Latifolia*), its flowers in bud resembling the iced gems we ate at birthday parties. I was lost in a secret world, listening to the birds and bees, hearing leaves rustle, watching the sunlight and shadow shift and dance on the trunks of trees and nobody knew I was there.

There were many secret spots in our garden- a glade of apple trees bordered on all sides by high hedges, another being the "vineyard" which my father planted within the walled garden, where I would sit for hours between the vines and write poetry, then there was a cave created by a large rhododendron, and finally a big beech tree down the end of a long and overgrown path. At the end of this whimsical path which took us past flowerbeds full of roses, we reached a clearing where the beech tree stood, all by itself, large and majestic. Under its spreading canopy of dripping leaves, bronzed in the autumn and strewn across the ground with the empty cases of abandoned beech nuts, I savoured the smell of damp leaves and earthy mulch.

I am making the garden sound so grand, but it really wasn't. Indeed, it was beautiful and well established, having a lot of lovely old oriental shrubs and trees planted at the time the house was built. It was beautiful but unkempt, an unruly whimsical garden most of which ran wild, a bit like its child and pet inhabitants, and was full of wildlife including snakes. We had no gardener to keep it in order and my father, of which gardening was just one of his many talents and hobbies, also had a very demanding full-time job and not many willing helpers. No larger than an acre, the garden was part of what was once a bigger plot shared with the house next door. Both that house and ours were built by two wealthy Edwardian spinster sisters in 1911 who had a house each, but after their deaths the garden was divided between the two properties by the presence of the existing wall (hence the "walled garden") and a large yew hedge.

Those were idyllic days, which perhaps elevates the garden in my mind's eye, and most of my rose-tinted memories of our house are in autumn. I remember sitting in the big bay window of the guest bedroom looking out at the changing colours of the trees and shrubs along our long driveway- the acers and maples- gold, red and orange, the sun cascading through the leaves to make them richer, more intense like flames before dying away to embers and the soft shadows of dusk when black-birds chipped their cosy echoing evening alarm calls before settling to roost. The vine around the window of the guest bedroom also turned to rich yellow and if one opened the window, one could reach out and pluck the sweet and succulent fruit, for these were desert grapes. The virginia creeper around my bedroom window was also a highlight of autumn as every year it turned to a deep, delicious red. I used to love the way it crept across the glass so that I felt like a princess enclosed in her secret castle tower and hated it when my father came to cut it back.

Autumn inspired me to decorate my room while my parents were away one weekend. I was sixteen and ready for something more sophisticated. Rummaging in the outhouse, amongst all the old paint pots and other articles of DIY, I found some matt white to de-pink the walls, adding a cream sponged effect over the top to mimic marble. I then painted frescoes freehand of trailing vines in gold, purple and black, evoking autumn and the sweet indulgence of grapes which

hung in heavy bunches in my father's vine-
yard outside. The result looked beautiful;
frescoed friezes, their abundant bunches
of grapes cascading sensually down the
walls. They caught the evening sunlight
flicking through the virginia creeper at my
window so that I could sit mesmerised by
the snaking ribbons of sunlight undulating
across my creations, causing the gold to
glow. And as the breeze tousled leaves and
branches outside, so shadows scampered
playfully across my newly painted walls
and I felt a delicious sense of security as the
day dipped down to dusk, imagining the
wild animals wandering in the shrubbery;
the badgers and foxes, the birds roosting
in the tall trees outside. I also dreamt of
sun-soaked vineyards on mellow autumn
evenings in Italy or France and yearned to
travel to them. My parents didn't object to
the frescoes, until they moved house five
years later and realised that I had painted
around all the furniture.

I remember one autumn at the beginning
of November when I was much younger,
and my brother and I decided to play
outside in the dark. At the bottom of the
garden, from where you could hardly see
the house, we peeped through the fence
at the cemetery which lay adjacent, we

might have even gone there. I certainly remember going there by day, walking over the spiky shells of sweet chestnuts which lay splayed open on the path, the scampering of squirrels in the undergrowth. We always managed to spook ourselves by day but on this eerie evening in November when a sharp chill crept out of the shadows and a mist was forming over surfaces, we thought of the cemetery over the fence and froze with fear. It is strange how children wilfully put themselves through this. It is almost as if they are putting themselves to the test, to see if they can conjure courage for real situations. Or perhaps in the days without X-box and other computerised thrills, we just enjoyed the adrenaline rush.

Apples

Two small girls emerge from the apple orchard, long blonde curls catching the sun's long licking rays, faces flushed and sheepish. Their pouched cheeks conceal a guilty secret, given away by fists clutching fruit, bright apples as red as their bulging cheeks. They stumble into the sunlight through twiggy shadows and a daze of dapples, into the strong sunshine of an autumn afternoon. Their father turns to scold them as if like Eve, they had eaten forbidden fruit. Although these are National Trust orchards and the fruit not free for all, I can understand the excitement and the allure of such tempting treats, the two girls scampering into the orchard to feast on the fruit, perhaps before their father had had time to tell them otherwise. Their guilty demeanours now show sorrow for being impulsive. One of them holds out an apple to her father with a trembling hand, her lip quivering, looking up at him with large, pleading, innocent eyes, as if this simple act of sharing will make everything better.

These young girls have their whole life ahead of them, their parents and everyone they have known still young. Despite being surrounded by death and decay as the leaves fall around them and the fruits ripen before rotting on the ground, they do not notice it, or if they do, they think of it in a different way, as I did then. My world as an adult is mellowing, maturing. I look at it with a certain sense of nostalgia as it takes on the tones of autumn. With exception of my grandparents, most of the people who have ever played an important part in my early life: my parents, brother, aunts, uncles, cousins and family friends are still here and all still a strong part of my existence, still linking me to childhood and its sweet security. And when I sense the mellow tones of autumn, a melody with beautiful harmonies and glowing warmth, they always draw my adult self like a moth to a window, to my family and home.

Back in the orchard, wasps buzz about the windfalls, the fermented fruit lacing the air with an aroma of alcohol. At home in two of my childhood gardens my father had an orchard. There was something soothing about collecting the fruit, different colours textures, shapes and scents. There was the cox with its beautiful blush and thick matt skin, the russets with their golden olive matted glow. Both of these varieties were carefully and meticulously wrapped individually in newspaper and stored in boxes in the outhouse for consuming at Christmas and through the winter. I was always a little disappointed how they lost their crisp sharpness and took on a mellow softness, an altogether more subtle, rich, aromatic and adult flavour which I failed to appreciate as a child. Nevertheless, I enjoyed the industry of bringing the apples into store, feeling like a useful cog in a wheel and part of the process. My parents bottled a lot of the apples which my mother made into pies and crumbles with the cooking varieties- large, waxy and often misshapen. I remember their rich fresh fruitiness as we cut and cored them, removing bruise and blemish and the brown holes where caterpillars had tunnelled into the fruit. My brother and I were always trying to find the culprit embedded inside. The cosy kitchen would hang heavy with the fruity sweet fragrance of stewed apple and cinnamon, and I felt overwhelmed by comfort and security sitting next to the Aga cooker at the heart of the house and sometimes stirring the pot of bubbling fruit.

It was in autumn also that the leaves on the vines turned delicious, dreamy shades of crimson and orange and fruit dripped in dewy clusters. First the picking, then the pressing. In our first year, when the vine-yard was young, my brother and I trod the grapes in a bucket, the soft and squidgy feeling flowing between our toes and under our nails, our feet looking bruised with purple juice, grape skin clinging in sticky patches. We were plastered up to our ankles, but it was fun. Again, I felt part of an organic process, a family venture initi-ated by my enterprising father, always full of interests and dreams, always embarking on exciting new projects and hobbies.

And as he lived his dreams, he encouraged my brother and I to become part of them, whether it was apple picking, raspberry picking, music making, gardening, DIY (the latter of which I have never been any good at) Each enterprise was a great and admirable adventure to a child. My mother's cooking, the preserving of autumn fruits with pickles and jams, bottling and stewing, the cooking of soups and stews and using nature's autumn produce also deeply influenced me and inspired me. Her creativity around the home, designing cushions and curtains from pieces of patchwork- pieces of the past transformed into something tangible, threaded with memories, made for a cosy and comfortable household. I am immensely grateful for the wonderful childhood which I so much appreciate and how it has made home so important to me.

The woodpile

There was something intriguing about the woodpile at the bottom of the garden. The damp resinous smell of chopped wet wood, tree rings alluding to time and age, the splintered shafts where some had been hacked across the grain. I would finger the bark feeling its rough contours, tracing patterns in its ridged surface, enjoying every undulation of the tree's tough skin. Beneath the looser bark, if one prized if off, lifting it like a lid, were a host of creepy-crawly creatures which ran scurrying for cover: woodlice, spiders, beetles, earwigs and tiny centipedes. They also made their homes beneath the logs and would run around in a frenzy if a log was lifted or rolled back. I always wondered how they managed to live out their lives without being squashed. The woodpile if it had been left a long time, would also act as host to fungi and slime moulds; some so small that they were hard to see; they formed in me a fascination for their alien worlds which I still hold today.

My father would often collect logs from the forest which lay adjacent to our garden, bundling them into a wheelbarrow and trundling them home through the garden gate which opened onto the forest path. He had an axe and would spend many a Saturday or Sunday afternoon in autumn chopping the logs to store for this season and for winter. He would wield the axe above his head, bringing it crashing down with a monumental thud. I loved the rhythmic sound of the axe chopping through the logs, the smell of freshly spilt wood as he tore through the grain and the satisfaction as a splintered chunk would fall with a thud on the ground beside him ready for the fire.

The wood burner would be lit in autumn as the days drew in and the nights grew chill. We would collect kindling from the forest; twigs and sticks which would be lit first with scrunched up newspaper. Once this was well alight, my father would add a log or two. There was a crackle, hiss and spit as the logs took to the flame, sometimes a little damp and hard to get going. The resinous smoky smell which they would exude while filling the room with warmth and the soft shapes infused by firelight was something I associated with home. I would watch the flames dancing and leaping like genies from a bottle, they would lick around the logs, tapering up. I fancied they had faces, sneering, jeering, jesting, devouring the wood with their long licking tongues and smoky breath. They were elves and pixies, folk of the forest, their playful patterns told fierce and fiery fairy stories. Firelight would wink on the walls and glow in the hearth. Sometimes it would spit a spark which my father would quickly extinguish by stamping on it with his slippered foot and us children would squeal with excitement. To avoid sparks, my father would pull up the front of the wood burner, leaving it a crack at the top to draw in a suction of air so that the fire inside would break into an almighty roar. When it was roaring sufficiently, he would close the front completely, opening the circular frontal vent with a metallic scrape to allow air inside. But if we wanted to watch the flames leap and see the sparks, he would leave the front open, sometimes applying a mesh fireguard, and adding a new log every time one had nearly burned away. The fire was greedy, guzzling the wood, the forage of the forest keeping us warm. The cat would curl up in front of the fire or tuck herself into the small space underneath the wood burner. The dog would stretch out on the hearthrug and go to sleep, both allowing the intense heat to soak into them. My parents would nod in their chairs, the fire producing a sleepy, after-supper atmosphere of extreme contentment. I would often sit with a book, my eyes often just skimming the pages as I became entranced by the wonderful atmosphere which my parents had created. My father would carefully put on a record, something classical, often opera. He would gently drop the stylus onto the band at the edge of the vinyl disc, its crackle stimulating a few seconds of anticipation. Then the music would start, surround sound through huge freestanding speakers, as if one were in a concert hall. The shape of the speakers resembled robots to us children, a large "body" topped with a smaller "head" around which we would sometimes tie a headscarf to make it look pretty. My father still swears by vinyl. Very often he would be asleep when the music had finished, and I would listen to the endless rhythmical thump and crackle of the stylus as it reached the end of the vinyl disc and was waiting to be gently levered off.

There is something primeval about sitting in front of a fire, something ancestral. Although environmentalists are now saying that we should no longer burn wood or have chimneys, and I do get their point, it is an ancient custom of drawing in away from the dark and cold and finding family bonding, a tradition which would be sorely missed. It was always very hard to prize oneself away from the fireside and make ones way up the staircase to bed. For outside that room everywhere else held a distinct chill. The only other source of relative heat in the house was the Aga. Stationed at the heart of the house in the breakfast room, it was an object of benevolence on cold, tired afterschool evenings. I would stand in front of it after walking home from school, watching my mother cook and generally getting in the way, hovering my hands above the plates, warming them. Sometimes I would even place my feet in the simmering oven!! My mum would bake bread and cook casseroles in the oven above it. She would also bring out pies and crumbles made with our autumn apples, steaming and sweet. She would make soup, pickles and preserves on the rings above, bottle fruit. She would also cook our every evening meal and often I helped, for this is how I learnt to cook.

After the evening meal or a large Sunday lunch we would retire to the fire to while away the time with a record and a book, hardly ever any television. But who needs television when you can watch the flickering flames of the fire dancing in the hearth and let your imagination run riot.

Collections

On my bookcase lies a large piece of ammonite found at the edge of a path in the Dorset countryside one walk during autumn. It is part of my much more extensive fossil collection; a fascination for fossils causing me since childhood to have always been on the subconscious look out for them nearly everywhere I go. Old habits die hard but have paid dividends and now my collection comprises fossils from several parts of the world where I have travelled, and of course from my home county Dorset which has allowed me to find the majority along its Jurassic coast. These fossils have come to gain the status of being some of my most treasured possessions.

I remember the air was distinctly cold in "sheep valley" as I like to call it, that day as I neared the end of a bracing walk in the Dorset Purbecks with my dad. The atmosphere as ever lay peaceful and still, layer upon layer of silence, a far cry from the shrill baby bleatings of lambs whose calls ricochet around the valley during springtime. Autumn hugged the air and drew it deep into itself, the stillness enhanced by the imperceptible movements of the sheep and their slow munching as they ripped at the grass. The small copse at the field edge, a delicious coppery colour, outside, on the edge, contained its own mystery. This haven for birds whose clandestine calls come from deep within the copse in springtime also lay silent, seemingly empty yet no doubt a shelter for wildlife.

As the piece of ammonite lay, its lazy ridges and smooth contours distinguishing it from the rough lumps of stone surrounding it, I was surprised to find such a fossil here. Autumn storms, ever more frequent, cause cliffs to tumble, exposing more fragments of fossils on beaches along the Jurassic coast, but not at the edge of pathways. I wonder if it had been dislodged by cows grazing the slopes above the path, causing it to be kicked down.

Despite the inclemency in weather often experienced at this time of year, it is probably the best time to be out finding fossils and I have spent many a gloomy grey day, taking my chances, muffled up against the autumn chill, scouring the cliff bases, picking my way through piles of pebbles and boulders and scraping through sand in certain areas where I know fossils are to be found.

It would seem that collecting or gathering, so synonymous with autumn, is not just confined to the season itself and is not a new phenomenon. My paternal grandparents like me, were incorrigible collectors and lovers of art, music, nature and history. Their house resembled a mini museum, a fascinating Aladdin's cave of wonder and delight, a treasure trove of display cabinets containing glass collections, endless pretty and impractical Victorian china (usually chipped and bought for a song at antiques markets), clocks that chimed at slightly different times (and which my grandfather had to go around and religiously wind, a daily ritual which would take some time to accomplish) and on the walls painting after painting ranging from contemporary watercolours bought as holiday souvenirs to a gallery of faded gilt frames and shadowy paintings by anonymous artists depicting what seemed to me then as the dim and distant past. These were collected by my great grandparents and passed down. They were bought for enjoyment rather than value, for none of them were worth very much. It was the joy of collecting that mattered, not investment. At the top of the stairs hung a portrait of my great grandfather gently looking down on us all.

All of this testifies to the eccentric English occupation of collecting things. My grandparents were strongly influenced by their Victorian parents and the Victorians and Edwardians of course were avid collectors; my local museum, the Russell-Cotes Museum in Bournemouth being a prime example. Within the walls of this on the cusp of Edwardian villa built by Sir Merton Russell-Cotes for his wife in 1901, is a treasure trove waiting to be discovered. 1901 was the year in which Queen Victoria died, and the house was completed. Therefore, it is perhaps technically Victorian, although much of what was assembled there would have been collected during the Edwardian era.

The house was built to house an entire art collection, and a collection of souvenirs brought back from around the world on great expeditions. One's eyes alight on an array of objects; weaponry, helmets, inlaid boxes, shells, stuffed animals, glass domes displaying beautiful butterflies, taxidermy, china, chiming clocks and the most impressive and extensive art collection making the whole house a gallery. Dark dreamy walls seem to yawn heavy opulence. This richness is not spared, lavished in the ubiquitous gilt friezes and ceiling decorations. Ticking clocks add to the somnolence. It is as if the house has lain like the sleeping beauty, lying on a luxurious chez longue through the entire 20th century while the outside world continues in bright crazy brilliance.

I want to cocoon myself in one of the glowing recesses wrapped warm in the indulgent atmosphere, one of headstrong, carefree leisure before the heavy oppression of World War one. This is a time-capsule, beautifully preserved, a turn-of the-century heart still beating with the ticking of the clocks. Yet as time ticks it seems to stand still, as if everything here has been trapped, locked up and preserved, a time-warp which draws one into itself and holds us captive here. Despite the dismal autumn weather outside, the rain slashing the windows and staining the sea and sky so that they merge as one, the house remains contained in a serene benevolence and faded glory. It is a happy place, and my heart holds several cherished memories of being blissfully happy here.

A Victorian gentleman's home in Bournemouth has also become a museum, a natural history museum. When entering the edifice, one is bowled over by the eccentricity which it exudes, a time capsule where one walks into a world of contagious curiosity, a Victorian world of academia and scientific research, reclusive, secret, shadowy. Victorian houses for me, always seem to hold this heaviness, but are forever intriguing. In the hallway stands a large dark wooden cabinet, full of seashells, large, exotic, intensely inviting and presumably collected on travels. It seems that all wealthy Victorians travelled. It was what one did if one had the means, a grand tour, a university of life for enriching and broadening the mind and for acquiring objects to prove status and the means and privilege to visit such remote and exotic climes, far out of the reach of the majority. The larger and more impressive articles which were collected, it would seem the better. Lord Elgin settled for nothing less than the marbles from the Parthenon (a present great source of contention), William Bankes at nearby Kingston Lacy took two years shipping an obelisk back from Egypt, and not satisfied with one, he shipped another, also filling an entire room with ancient Egyptian artefacts and bringing entire ceilings from palaces back from Italy. It seemed as if there was no limit as to what could be collected and brought back. My experience of collecting while travelling was a woven silk badge to sew onto my rucksack to show where I had been, a postcard to stick in a scrap-book, ephemera such as the wrappers from bars of continental chocolate and entrance tickets to caves and museums. I would also fill my pockets with cowries and carnelians scavenged from the beaches in northern

France and West Runton respectively.

When not on holiday, I collected Victorian memorabilia, which my grandmother supervised and encouraged as an extension of her own collections and passions, and as an excuse to go to antiques markets and find me treasures. Then there were the fossils, antique letters and postcards and the ubiquitous books (the latter of which my grandparents also heartily helped me with.) My collections pale into insignificance however, when compared to Victorian collections, which were taken to a new level with the height of the extravagance they pursued.

The Bournemouth Natural Science Society museum is far from extravagant or opulent in comparison with the collections at Kingston Lacy, but there is something warming and endearing about it. I peruse the glass cases of rare, beautiful butterflies from south America and other places, pinned in neat rows, their large wings iridescent and delicately patterned and am grateful to the person who brought them back, for I would never have the opportunity to see such beautiful creatures in real life. We walk across creaky floorboards, discovering more curiosities; a whole room dedicated to seeds and exotic plants, an

Egyptian room, a room full of fossils, the usual taxidermy so popular in Victorian times. There are experts in every room to talk to us, academics who have spent a lifetime pursuing something obscure and niche, such as restoring old microscopes or studying ancient seeds.

Sitting in the corner of a room full of old glass bottles used in chemistry, is a skeleton. I wonder if he will make a proper appearance for Halloween which is coming soon. The skeleton, a male, used for purposes of anatomy back in the day, seems quite comfortable sitting there minding his own business, although his owner says that as his wife does not appreciate having a skeleton on display at home, he (the skeleton) is locked in a cupboard there. "Everyone has a skeleton in their cupboard", he jokes, as if it is an everyday occurrence. Maybe not in a cupboard but my father certainly had one when he was a medical student back in the 1960s. Its abode was the top bunk in the spare bedroom at my grandparent's house and when not being used for anatomical purposes, wore my father's crash helmet. My mum recounts the sleepless nights she spent with the skeleton rattling around above her every time she turned over, as she slept in the bottom bunk when, before she married my dad, she went to stay.

By far the best example of a Victorian gentleman's collection must be the Pitt-Rivers Museum in Oxford. Henry-Augustus Pitt-Rivers, sometimes known as the father of modern archaeology, is an unsung hero in my part of the world. After serving in the army, he inherited a vast estate on Cranborne Chase in Dorset from where he conducted extensive and meticulous archaeological research, cataloguing and measuring all finds and leaving copious drawings of artefacts and investigations. He was also something of a philanthropist, establishing the very popular Larmer Tree pleasure gardens on his estate for the general public to enjoy. It included a bandstand, golf, an open-air theatre, picnic areas, an art gallery, Indian houses and a small zoo amongst other attractions. He also opened a small museum of local archaeology in Farnham, near Larmer Tree, the contents of which have now been divided between the Salisbury and South Wiltshire Museum in Salisbury and the Pitt-Rivers Museum in Oxford.

Pitt-Rivers' curiosity for anthropology did not begin in Dorset, however. For many years he had collected while travelling around the world. In 1884, he donated his entire collection of 20,000 objects to the University of Oxford for educational purposes. The museum, now housing half a million objects, is a complete delight. Appearing haphazard in their glass cases, the volume of objects can be overwhelming, and I walk around in serendipitous fashion, not knowing where to start and when to stop. There is a freedom in this spontaneity, not having to follow set out routes and wandering at whim through a maze of fascination. I could quite happily spend all day in here, lost amongst the eclectic displays, embraced by an environment in which I feel totally at home. Here I have travelled back in time, my eyes alighting on and devouring numerous curiosities and it is hard to tear myself away. While William Bankes might have imported obelisks from Egypt, Pitt-Rivers brought back a totem pole which towers up through the centre of the museum at 11.36 meters tall and carved from a red cedar tree. There seems to be no limit as to what objects Victorian collectors would bring home.

There is something lovely about collections, the ad hoc serendipity, the not knowing what you might find. Half looking, as ever, for fossils, I never expected to find one in a forest of all places, but out walking one afternoon I happened to look down in my customary manner and there it was staring up at me on the forest track, a complete stone sea-urchin, heart-shaped and star encrusted of the *Micraster* genus. It absolutely made my day, the sense of excitement, of wonder, of being in the right place at the right time, of knowing that if I hadn't found it, it might have been lost, the wonder at its provenance. These and many other thoughts continually spring into mind when collecting something ancient or old. One man's rubbish is certainly another man's treasure, and this cannot be truer than for the people who go mudlarking in the river Thames. A permit is now required for this activity which apparently becomes more popular in autumn as this is when the Thames, being a tidal river, retreats, exposing more mud. Mudlarking is a form of archaeology in that the mudlarkers piece together the past through the artefacts which they find and therefore develop a comprehensive social history of London.

I have never personally been mudlarking, although it is something that seriously appeals. Perhaps it will become a future pastime. For the present there is, for me however, nothing much better than perusing an antique shop, a junk shop or a second-hand bookshop. Antiques markets are the most satisfying. There you can buy chipped china and silver-plated cutlery for a song. I have a box full of vintage china which my grandmother collected for me, pretty plates and china cups. I also have a shoebox of old black and white postcards, old letters... collecting is an addiction. I always come back from a second-hand bookshop with a new addition for the pile on the floor as my books have outgrown any sensible space.

I believe that collecting runs deep in our DNA. It is something which satisfies us all, the thrill of the search, the feeding of fascinations, the act of finding and owning something special which feeds into the imagination or reflects our identity in some way. I conducted a small survey at work as we have a range of colleagues from different parts of the world. It seems that everybody collected something when they were a child but as adults, only a third of us do. Most of my non-British colleagues said that collecting was also popular in their countries, which proves my point.

Recently I read an article which claimed that prehistoric people also collected things. Fossilised spiral shells were found in caves in northern Spain. As they had not been modified in any way to make tools or jewellery, and from the amount that were found, fifteen in total, archaeologists believe that these were collected for being attractive and ornamental. I wonder perhaps as well because they were mysterious. It suggests that people were curious about them, finding them compelling, that they found wonder in nature and perhaps in natural history. The shells could also have been regarded as symbolic or magic, but they could equally, claim archaeologists, have been collected as ornaments because they were aesthetically pleasing, and people enjoyed finding and keeping them. They even think that prehistoric children might have collected them.

I imagine these ancient people secure in their caves, the light licking into recesses, shadows wandering up walls and firelight leaping across faces, faces full of wonder, watching so intently, finding forms in the flames, shapes and genies, faces and patterns. They might have been mesmerised, just as we might be today sitting in front of the fire on a chill autumn evening. These ancient firelit faces found interest in antiquity just as we do today, they peered at fossils trying to find meaning in their peculiar patterns and shapes. Perhaps they wondered why these shells of stone didn't break as others did. Did they know how they were formed and how they came to be? I am sure these people were much more sophisticated and intelligent than we like to think, we who arrogantly accept that progress is linear with time ever marching forward towards greater sophistication and that we are somehow superior.

I believe these people were skilled with bare hands and with the same technology and opportunities that we have today, would have been equally capable and knowledgeable. Or perhaps they were even more capable then than we are today, given their technological limitations. Technology can make us lazy, taking away our skills, for who today could have built Stonehenge or the Pyramids or any of the beautiful British cathedrals without algorithms or computers to design and measure and draw? How could we construct them today without the aid of diggers and cranes? I feel we have lost something of ourselves and that although time never stands still, it is important to ground ourselves in its time-lessness and reconnect with what we have lost.

GARDENS

I love gardens in autumn; flowers rich in colour and texture- dahlias of all shape and size; rich reds and copper colours, yellow, cream and pink. In early autumn one can still see roses, hot lips, red hot pokers and Michaelmas daisies vying for colour amidst a myriad berries; the yellow or deep orange of Pyracanthas, the red of Cotoneasters and sometimes even the purple of *Callicasta*, an ornamental berry see in gardens and beautiful beside grasses, the latter glanced by the sun so that its soft backlight sets them trembling on a misty morning. In the pale sunlight, an autumn garden can look ethereal, webbed with mist. Such dreamy days follow clear nights when the moon is bright and strong.

The vegetable garden is also at its best in autumn with rainbow chard topping the tops. Squashes and pumpkins in weird and wonderful shapes, colours and forms; some ornamental and some edible. As well as these, there are the apple-laden trees and the red crab apples which grow wild in the hedgerows.

As well as fresh produce, autumn is a time for preserving for winter. I remember local women in a Turkish village near where I used to live, with piles of tomatoes, making a tomato sauce, capturing the sunlight of summer with the sweet rich freshness of tomatoes and all their vitamins to be savoured during the winter months. They did this outdoors, a community activity, working together in order to bottle the sheer volume of fruit. Sometimes the tomatoes were mixed with peppers and aubergines. The later would also be dried and hung on strings, seen in the courtyards of some old village houses.

At this time of year, olives would also be picked and preserved. Trees are often shaken to release the fruit which is caught in large nets. Olives are preserved in olive oil and brine with different seasonings. It is a labour-intensive job but in Turkish culture, everything is prepared in bulk. Families are large and extended and need to be fed throughout the winter. Jars of preserves and bottles are stored on balconies. It is something traditional in every culture, the act of preserving, fermenting, keeping the freshness of summer and the bounty of autumn fruit in jars.

In my own family, apples are stewed and bottled, chutneys are made and jams. Although many jams come from summer fruits there are those which can be made of fig or quince, orange or lemon, which are more autumnal in their flavour and association. Autumn is the time in Turkey when the figs are ripe, dripping their delicious sweetness like honey when the fig splits to reveal its seeded insides. The orange harvest usually starts in about September with early varieties. The Spanish Seville orange being more of a bitter variety, makes marmalade which is rich and tangy to the taste.

Stourhead

Although there are many National Trust gardens vying for autumn supremacy, Stourhead is local and therefore one which I have experienced much more often than some of the others.

Towering trees provide a cascade of colour which lingers in the lake in a myriad reflections and refractions of light. Ducks cruise, creating currents, a spectrum of streamers weaving in their wake, their beaks bantering with what seems like laughter. I watch one of their feathers float and drift away dreamily as time takes it, a feather so light that it barely makes a mark in the meniscus. A leaf likewise lingers; carmine, palmate, fallen from one of the many acers at the water's edge. It floats, fused with the colour reflected beneath it, carmine on cantaloupe, crimson fraying into flames at the edges of the lake where the water laps and lilts. The ducks appear to be in paradise as they cruise up and down, drakes with their green glint of plumage vocal in their iridescence, following the females less colourful yet intricately marked; understated beauties luring the males. Ducks follow seasonal monogamy, which means they change their partners every breeding season. Some birds mate for life.

On a beautiful day and with the right conditions, the brilliant blaze of colour in the tree canopy at Stourhead can be truly breathtaking, reminding me of the autumn colours in Canada. One particular year, I think it was 2007, Stourhead was spectacular, the dry summer followed by an autumn of cold nights gave the ideal conditions for trees to turn colour more intensely. All deciduous trees photosynthesise and the chlorophyll (green pigment) in the leaves acts with spring and summer sunshine to create sugars for the tree. When temperatures cool and the days become shorter, chlorophyll production is decreased and eventually stopped and leaves then reveal the carotenes (oranges and yellows) which are present within them. Other plant species, such as maples and acers, manufacture anthocyanins in early autumn in response to a buildup of sugars in the leaves. These chemicals produce the purples, crimsons and intense scarlets so pronounced in these types of trees. That is what makes Stourhead so richly colourful. Acers and other ornamental plants became very popular in gardens from the 18th century all the way through to the late 19th and early 20th centuries when Japanese gardens were also the vogue.

The garden at Stourhead is essentially a landscaped 18th century classical design with its manmade water features, temples and grottoes, the iconic classical temple of Apollo, used in the 18th century as an alfresco dining room with views across the water, framing the scene. It is the first view that most people see as they walk into the garden.

The garden was designed by "Henry the magnificent" (Henry Hoare II) who, according to the National Trust, wanted to create a classical garden which reflected his world travels. At this time, in the 18th century, with the increase in global exploration, it was popular for plants to be collected and brought back to the UK.

The results of such a collection, continued by Hoare's successor and grandson Sir Richard Colt Hoare, can be seen extensively in the garden at Stourhead which listed at that time, 90,000 trees. Indeed, the densely forested slopes which surround the lake seem to stretch forever upwards. Following the leafy paths which wander these slopes and skirt around the periphery of the lake, our gaze takes us ever higher up the mighty trunks of giant redwoods, and across, peering through the skeletal shells of rhododendrons which have created caves of branches under which children play. Sir Richard Colt Hoare was not only a collector of trees but also of Pelargoniums of which, according to the Trust, he collected and propagated 600 varieties. He was also an antiquarian and archaeologist who made valuable contributions to local archaeology and a collector of books, many of which remain in his impressive library.

We walk out of the garden through fields leading up to King Alfred's tower, a 18th century folly standing on top of Kingsettle hill and erected by Henry Hoare II in commemoration of the fact that King Alfred apparently raised his standard here in 870 AD. It rises austere and somewhat sinister in the quiet autumn air, a peaceful place which has seen so much before. The fields are flanked by beech trees which blaze in the brilliant sunshine, the path running beneath them crackling with beechmast. Ambling through these fields full of gently grazing cows and a rather formidable looking bull, I figure these are National Trust livestock so we have to trust that the bull will be well-behaved and not chase after us and that his harem will not follow suit. They all seem unphased, he assuming the role of a gentle giant who appears to be more interested in grazing.

Stourhead is lovely in autumn, the gentle warmth of the last vestiges of summer sun stealing the shorter days compliment the warmth of the trees' vibrant colours. Trees in their final moments of glory before they go into a state of torpor, as if in hibernation, shut against the winter's cold.

Kingston Lacy

As a volunteer for the National Trust, I have come to know Kingston Lacy extremely well, working there through the seasons. My favourite time in the gardens here is always autumn when the sun casts long lazy shadows between the trees and the acers in the Japanese garden take on an intensity all of their own.

The Japanese tea garden is an example of a Victorian and Edwardian craze for establishing a little of the orient back home. At this time, not only plants such as azaleas, acers and rhododendrons were cultivated in many of Britain's gardens, but also those specifically Japanese in style. Kingston Lacy is no exception. The small garden with a lily pond, winding path, and pagoda, is flanked by acers and other asian plants. I watch the sun striking through the leaves, piercing colours layered with light and shadows. Bamboos stand straight and dense along the path. Their sculpted style, architectural, erect. Serried ranks in lines, lines both vertical and horizontal, a contrast of colours in subtle greens, beige, brown, paper-like leaves rustling.

This is the main feature of the gardens in autumn, the other parts pale into autumn; deciduous trees losing leaves; the horse chestnut with its spiky seedcases, the oak and beech. Fungi flourish in the woodland glades and along the path where old tree trunks lie recumbent, rotting, providing nutrients for other life. These are golden days of dreamy lingering light. Days cut short as nights draw in and the colours contract into themselves and into the darkness of dusk.

Bournemouth pleasure gardens

It is often harder to gauge a sense of season in a city. One has to walk further, longer to understand the change. Bournemouth's pleasure gardens were created by the Victorians when Bournemouth was at the height of its popularity as an elegant seaside resort. At the beginning of the 19th century, pine trees were planted extensively on the native heathland. These trees still stretch along the clifftops and along the shaded streets giving Bournemouth a nostalgic, restful air of ease, faded opulence and carefree comfort, or so it used to be. Now one has to switch off from the present if you want to glean a sense of the past. It is only felt in a few secluded secret places such as at the Russell-Cotes Museum, at Alum Chine when golden sunshine slants between the pine trees and a breeze stirs gently in their branches, or further into the gardens towards Coy Pond. Bournemouth has lost a lot of its charm and, although still a popular place to retire and to go on holiday, has many social problems.

Out of season the town claims back some of its quiet sense of nostalgia. A walk through the gardens in autumn connects one to the season, squirrels scurrying in the pine needles, sitting up straight to eat pinenuts and then digging avidly and furiously to bury what they can't consume. In early autumn the maple trees flame with beautiful colours and later the deciduous trees turn delicious shades of gold and yellow. One can walk for a couple of miles along by the Bourne stream and feel the flavour.

Out in the square, a street preacher stands amidst stray swirling leaves imploring everyone in this time of world change to seek first the kingdom of God. It is true that the world is changing at unprecedented and alarming rates and people are asking questions as to why and what is happening. We try to explain things through climate change and bad governments, we try to get quick feel-good fixes, but I feel there is much more to it than that. The American word for autumn, fall, might even sum it up. As autumn should be a time of survival, of collecting and gathering in, of defeating death physically, his message seems to resonate spiritually.

I wander through the gardens and find a quiet place to sit and read beneath a tree. The sun is still strong as it is October, a savour of summer lingering in the last of the verbena which pushes its purple profusion of tall spiky arms ever upwards.

Bees are still out and about nectaring on these final flowers. Butterflies join them, usually the Red Admirals, which seem to be the sole survivors of the summer still out on the wing. They especially seek out the ivy flowers, loved by honeybees and wasps, the final offering of energising nectar to pollinators to store before they hibernate.

All hibernating animals will be using autumn's bounty to fatten up before their long winter sleep. It is survival. Likewise, the birds make the most of the autumn berries before the winter bites. Sadly, many will die if the winter is cold or if storms break out. We cannot be prepared for every eventuality, but we can prepare for what we know is inevitable.

Harvest

The greater garden outside our own private spaces is surely the fields and it is at no other time more than this that we celebrate the fruits of farmer's labour. Perhaps it is not so fashionable now, but certainly was when I was at primary school. The church would be decorated with flowers and produce in beautiful arrangements, sheaves of wheat, dried grasses, sunshine slanting through stained glass, causing Norman pillars and thick stone sills to be bathed in beautiful colours. The flowers would catch the radiant backlight and seem to glow.

At school every year we would bring in tokens of fresh food and take part in a harvest service of thanksgiving. Piles of pumpkins, squash, courgettes, carrots, cabbages, tomatoes and all other things imaginable would jostle for space on trestle tables in the school hall. Once I felt ashamed for bringing in a tin of sweetcorn as I had forgotten to bring produce from our garden, for every year I would bring some leeks or a cabbage or something home grown. We would sing the harvest hymn *We plough the fields and scatter*. It was a hymn of gratitude and as children it made us thankful as well as learning about where our food actually came from. Apparently, many modern children think that apples come from Tesco!

The harvest festival for the church holds a deeper more spiritual meaning of gratitude. For it is also about gratitude for God's provision of salvation and redemption, bringing about a spiritual regeneration, a metamorphosis. A similar metaphor is shown with the fishermen James and John who as well as being disciples, caught fish to earn their livelihood. They are described as fishers of men, for as they preached, they brought in a harvest of souls.

The harvest festival is a tradition of thanksgiving and spiritual significance for the church, but it is also an act of charity. Much of the produce is sold and the money made will be donated. Sometimes food is collected for the local foodbank. It is therefore a bringing together of people for a good cause, appreciating the combined effort of community and the bounty which autumn brings.

Other countries and cultures hold similar festivals bringing together communities in gratitude and celebration. The famous festival of Thanksgiving in Canada and the United States is a national holiday which celebrates the bringing in of harvest. Sukkot similarly is the Jewish festival which falls in autumn and not only celebrates harvest but the period of Exodus when the people were led out of Egypt by God to safety. In China and other Asian countries, the harvest is celebrated around September with the moon festival and the making of moon cakes and in African countries such as Ghana and Nigeria, yam festivals are held at the beginning of autumn with much singing and dancing in hope that the crop will grow and avert famine.

Finder's Keepers

The idea of ploughing the fields mentioned in the hymn that was so often sung at school does not necessarily occur in autumn. On intensive farms, however, I have seen a crop harvested in early autumn, the field then ploughed and ready to be sown again in spring. In the country museum at Braemore, Hampshire, amongst the vintage tractors and the centuries old corn dollies (intricately woven to hang in barns and farmhouses to invite a good harvest) an interesting selection of ploughs is on display. Originally pulled by horses which walked up and down the length of the field, the plough changed shape and size as farming became more mechanised and modernised.

This machinery in whatever form was, however, responsible for profoundly changing the nature of the landscape and destroying much of our native downland and pasture, turning it over to fields for food. Writers such as W. H Hudson, speaking out at the beginning of the 20th century, and H. J. Massingham, an admirer of Hudson who writing in the 1930s, reiterates much of what he said, decry this destruction. According to Hudson, the agricultural labourers who worked on the flinty fields, which were once chalk down-land, were constantly finding fossilised echinoids, presumably turned up with the disturbance of the soil and the cut of the plough. Not knowing what they were but perhaps being attracted to their pentam-eral design, these labourers kept them as amulets, placing them in doorways and on window ledges, attaching wonder to them in the form of superstition and magic.

Similar fossils have been found inside bronze age tumuli in Britain and at ancient burial sites in many parts of the world, suggesting that prehistoric people were perhaps captivated by their symmetry and associated them with some kind of mysticism.

The most exciting find in Britain, says palaeontologist Kenneth McNamara in his book *The star crossed stone*, was that of the Dunstable downs in the Chiltern hills in 1887 by Worthington George Smith, a man who I would have loved to have met. A frustrated artist who couldn't get his career off the ground, Worthington Smith resorted to a fascination in fungi, which he assiduously collected every autumn, studied meticulously and drew in detail. From his tenacious and perhaps foolhardy research, conducted very much by trial and error, and luckily not to his detriment, he wrote and illustrated a definitive guide to fungi asserting which were and were not edible. He was also an amateur archaeologist, invited to excavate several tumuli at Dunstable which had been destroyed by the plough. Worthington states that in one barrow he found the rather squashed skeletal remains of a teenage boy, the other offered the bones of a young woman and infant child surrounded by a collection of 200 fossilised echinoids, suggesting some spiritual association with these fossils.

Did these people make some connection with the star on the urchin to the stars in the sky? Ancient people were much more in tune with the night sky and its signs than we are today. It is certainly thought that the ancient Egyptians used the five-pointed star symbol in association with the night sky, according to McNamara. He also states that ancient Egyptians believed that their Pharaohs became stars in the sky after death, an interesting metamorphosis. I wonder if stars could have been associated with life after death in other ancient cultures. Stars or suns with multiple radial points have certainly been shown on ancient Greek goldware found in tombs. However, it is not certain that bronze age Britons made the same associations. Stars in the night sky do not necessarily look as if they have points, it is only the way they twinkle through the atmosphere which gives us this impression. Therefore, we perhaps shouldn't assume, from our modern perspective, that they held the same beliefs as those in other faraway cultures or indeed that they held the same associations with shapes and heavenly bodies as we do today.

McNamara maintains that bronze age people perhaps shared similar beliefs with northern European cultures and that associations with fossil echinoids based in Norse mythology may be more likely. Thor, the god of the sky, thunder, weather and crops was thought to rain down fossil urchins during a thunderstorm. The fossils in fields were thought perhaps to magically ensure a good harvest of crops, meeting the physical, rather than the spiritual needs of agricultural communities and their reliance on the provision of food to keep them alive. Fossil echinoids have also been found buried in the walls of Romano British houses near to where I live, presumably as some sort of protection, implying that later cultures continued to consider these fossils as apotropaic.

Ancient people were perhaps unaware as to what fossils really were and there certainly seems to have been almost a fear of them up until the 18th century when scientists dared to suggest that they might be the remains of extinct species. Mary Anning, another local legend of my part of the world, who found the first complete Ichthyosaur on the beach at Lyme Regis in 1811 was not necessarily aware of the significance of what she had discovered. She collected what she called "curios" to make a living. Ammonites in those days were called "snake stones", and belemnites "devil's fingers" or "thunderbolts". All of them perhaps were used as lucky charms rather than appreciated for their antiquity and the fact that these species were now extinct. Echinoids were apparently known as thunderstones, still believed to have been hurled down to earth by the Viking god Thor. Even up until the 1920s they were customarily placed on window ledges and in doorways to protect a house from being struck by lightning. It is ironic that Mary Anning herself survived a lightning strike as a child.

Hearing that echinoids can be found in fields was like music to my ears. Ever since I learnt this, I have kept my eyes peeled every time I go walking through the fields in areas of chalk downland near to where I live in Dorset. I had been looking out for them for the best part of a decade and never found one in a field until a walk which went wrong. With hindsight it was completely fortuitous. Still down in Dorset, taking the Purbeck Way the wrong way by accident, I found myself following the path around a farm and continuing down beside fields to a wooded hollow. I am not endowed with an innate sense of direction at the best of times, in fact I would say that it is severely lacking, and with my internal compass confused, I was just about to berate myself for not heading towards the sea when I took stock and said to myself with a determined and non- defeatist attitude of curiosity "I am taking this path now. No turning back, let's see where it leads." I also wondered subconsciously if there would be any fossils. This thought has been so ingrained in my mind since childhood that it never really registers, but this time as I strode along I was conscious that I was on the Jurassic coast and although I wasn't usually lucky, there was every reason why I should be. I even said it out loud. Perhaps this was providential because only two minutes later I spied a large round stone at the edge of the public footpath striped with the star of a sea urchin. My excitement instantly soared to new heights, heart pounding. It was one of those eureka moments of finding something that you least expect and have always wanted to find, and because you have been searching for it for so long that you have almost given up hope, it gives exquisite joy.

However near to home it is, an outing is always an adventure if you seek out its possibilities and I appreciate the beauty of walking with an open mind, always paying close attention to surroundings, stimulating curiosity. Wherever you are, however mundane the setting, you never know what you are going to see, experience or find and these simple pleasures are always for me the most thrilling.

In dreamy disbelief I picked up the fossil-ised urchin, placing it in my palm, letting my fingers wrap around it. It was real, a dream only in the sense that it was a dream come true; weighty and cold, solid, tanta-lising, mysterious and beautiful. I found so many dimensions of wonder and pleasure just by holding it in my hand and contem-plating its age and identity, for I have never seen such a large and highly domed fossil-ised urchin, reminiscent of a small home-made hot cross bun (which always rise into a beautiful sugared dome unlike the flat flabby shop varieties). These urchins were actually known as fairy loaves, according to Worthington. The star shape which decorated the dome and is common to all urchins extended down the sides and I could trace lines of spines along its base. I never cease to marvel at the design in nature, the symmetry of the simple star, reminiscent of a snowflake, except that the urchin star has five sides and a snowflake always six. It sometimes snows in autumn.

As I put the fossilised urchin in my pocket (it was, after all found on a public path), I saw that it had been damaged, one part of it cut off, I imagine lost to the plough as the break was clean, unless it was damaged at death. But it was still beautiful, perfect in its imperfection because it told a story. I put my hand back into my pocket, feeling its presence, reassuring myself that it was still there and relishing the pros-pect of spending some time later quietly perusing the fascinating website of the British Geological Society (to which I am a fairly frequent visitor) to identify its exact extinct species.

Chalkland areas were once areas of sea. The chalk being the result of crushed shells and calcium deposits. I wondered if this urchin lived up here, feeding off the gooey seabed so many millennia ago. I am staggered to think that it has been here all through history, from the beginning of written records. How did it stay hidden for all those centuries? How was it not found thousands of years ago hiding out its years until I just picked it up off the border of a field which must have been ploughed so many times before. That in itself is the biggest wonder and mystery to me. I imagine that the maize had been harvested a few weeks before, as many maize cobs still littered the ground, pressed into the mud, and with the harvest of the maize the field stood empty, exposing stones which were more easily seen, stones which had hidden for millennia, finally lifted and turned by the plough preparing the land for harvest.

AWAY-AUTUMN ADVENTURES

Change brings with it excitement and anticipation at times and autumn has always been a time to travel. In hot countries the autumn temperature is not as fierce and unbearable as summer, yet warmer than in the UK. Autumn is traditionally the start of a new academic year and with the autumn term, as a teacher abroad, that always meant the start of something new.

Greece

Light lingered over the Parthenon, morning light melting into the stone. Caryatids stayed sleeping in the shadows around the porch of the Erectheon, only to be woken by the spill of the sun fingering their faces with golden light, drawing them from their dreams so that they seemed to come alive. We arrived early in the morning before the world had really woken. The sun seemed to touch the Parthenon and then the Acropolis, both being at the highest point over Athens, while the city still slumbered in the penumbra below. There were no tourists here yet and we watched the waking Parthenon like a revelation unveiled by the break of day.

The air is still warm in Greece in September, more like summer. And yet there is still that feeling of returning to the old routine as groups of post summer holiday school children in smart uniforms bundle onto buses and the world yawns into action. Soon there will be a distinct honking of horns in the city below, the street cafes where people savour shots of strong Greek coffee and eat hot pastries will fill the air with their fragrance and stray cats will take their winding, sinuous walks around the table legs, waiting for titbits.

Away from the hub, history is ever present along with timelessness and the chance to dream. The forested areas below the Acropolis seem trapped in a time warp, a slice of nature singing with bright birdsong within in a sprawl of concrete which stretches seemingly forever under a canopy of smog. As a teenager on a 6th form school trip, I attended an open-air theatre production at the foot of the acropolis, sitting outside in the early autumn heat as if it were still summer; a sol et lumiere which captured my imagination and encapsulated the whole Athenian experience. For Athens is not a beautiful city, and it is easy to feel overwhelmed there, but it holds a cluttered, chaotic charm; one which is sporadic and haphazard, happy go lucky and fancy free.

Delphi dripped in dreamy morning light before the first tourist buses rolled up. Again we arrived early; sunlight spilling over a beautiful undulating wooded landscape, in the distance the slick of sea. Trees had not quite turned then, birds still sang. In early autumn it is still like summer but quieter, more pensive. The heat of the day rises with the hours and yet in those early amber moments one feels the seasons turning.

It was the same in evening when one became aware of longer shadows. Driving through villages in the Peloponnese, where sunlight sank into the rough textures of crumbling plastered walls and small single-storey houses with pitched tile rooves were wound with trailing vines. Grapes hung succulently blushing in the sinking sun. Old people sat outside the front of their houses at plastic tables on plastic chairs, smoking, drinking, gossiping, traditional men in cloth caps, shabby, dusty, a wealth of experience in their furrowed faces, the women overweight, dressed in simple skirts and tops, clothes non-descript. Their faces kind, crinkly, motherly. The villages were often places where children ran free. We would call them "free range children" back in the UK. Safe communities where there was no threat and where everyone could be involved in village life, the olive picking, the grape harvest and the figs so soft that they split and the honeyed juices ran out onto your fingers. Melting in the mouth, the velvety skin and the soft, sweet centre which is home to a type of wasp whose microscopic embryo developing inside the fruit is inadvertently consumed.

In Samos the villages seemed to be happy places filled with laughter. Children roamed the streets at night while their parents sat talking in tavernas under strings of lights. Outside these hilltop villages under the stars the milky way stretched across the sky and owls hooted from the forest where we had been walking all day. There is so much hiking to be had on Samos, the forest trails wending their way through the trees which were just starting to turn in mid-September and were filled with captivating birdsong, some of which I didn't recognise from home. After at least a 20-kilometre hike, it was custom to stop in one of the small mountain villages for an early evening meal, usually staying until well after the sun had set and the moon had climbed high above the village. Windows winked warmly in the old Greek houses; crumbling plaster and peeling paint, wrought iron balconies, wooden shutters and tiled roofs. The laughter of children cut through the drone of adult conversation, while outside this glowing microcosm, the backdrop of the night with its steady hum of cicadas remained a mystery, compelling and deep. So it would remain until the call of the cockerel serenaded the dawn and kept up his momentum most of the day. Infused in a dreamy somnolence of the out of season, the weather still warm, Greece seemed to glow. We shared tavernas with locals. Music bright and always optimistic flowed across to the expanse of seashore and dissipated into the evening where the sea quiet and restful spilled onto the stones, the only sound being the rhythmic wash of its waves and the bony clattering of pebbles as the undertow sucked them back into the deep.

During my teaching days I often walked at Meteora when the trees were turning, and the autumn air was laced with chill. I climbed long tracks up to the summits. It was now November and the forested flanks of the steep rocks topped by medieval monasteries turned to rich shades of orange, yellow, ochre and umber which blended beautifully with the dreamy, smoky purple shades of the sleeping plains and valleys beneath. Villages at the base of the Meteora were preparing for winter. Woodsmoke hung on the air and chickens strutted and pecked in the roadside. The local taverna where the more elderly locals sat, smoked, and watched the world go by, prepared comforting soups and warm mezes eaten with freshly baked bread. They seemed to be already slowing down for winter, but then life was always slow there. A world away from technology and from the world itself, or so it seemed then. It too will have surely changed now.

Change is inevitable and in those times of travel, either living and working abroad or visiting on autumn holidays, the change was new, exciting, every day an adventure, a perpetual holiday. There was not an opportunity to feel homesick as every new day was different, exacerbated by the autumn colours and the change in temperature as the days drew darker. I worked in a mountain village not far from the Meteora and as the nights drew in and I worked late at the village school, I loved to sit with the classroom window open marking exercise books after the children had left (and more often writing as I was so inspired!), inhaling the last lingering flavours of the day and drinking in the delicious dream of dusk. It was a tonic so sustaining that although I felt far away from home, there was nowhere else I wanted to be at that moment in time. I was inspired by the colours of the trees on the mountainside as they slipped away to monochrome and became silhouettes before a backdrop of stars. From the depths of the forest came the haunting cries and shrieks of little owls, creating a deep sense of comfort, stimulating the senses to become captivated.

Sometimes curiosity would make me take a torch and go out into the night, to become immersed in it. I would wander down the road to the ancient bridge which straddled the river, the water thick and pure, chattering across stones in the starlight while the silhouettes of those intriguing nighttime wooded mountains towered above. Lost in awe, in timelessness. There was something so still, solid and soothing and yet so animated and tangible, with the feel in Greece that everything is ancient. This scene had stood the same for centuries, the river continually taking its course, the cycle of the seasons, the turning of the leaves to autumn and the day to night.

My view of living in Greece is perhaps coloured by the autumn, the positive enriching experiences I had working there, but I felt that even though there was poverty and economic hardship, people in these villages seemed sustained. They lived simple contented lives in jovial close communities of extended families and friends who supported each other. In the Greek village where I taught, everyone knew each other and children would happily play in any space while the women worked together, bottling, pickling, preserving the harvest just as they did in Turkey. Even in the cities, Greek housewives will buy kilos of vegetables from the market and spend their days and hours preparing pickles and sauces, cracking and marinading olives just as we preserve things in our kitchens here. With the absence of refrigeration in the past, which also meant that meat had to be hung or dried (octopus are still seen hanging to dry in the sun on Greek islands) and fish would be salted. It would therefore seem, as I said previously, that preserving is an ancient cross-cultural tradition of sustenance and survival, a preparation for the winter months when food is scarce, the provision of love and care, of close communities where people look out for each other. In this sense in Greece at least, nothing has changed.

Ohi day

October 28th, Ohi day, a day when the Greeks remember Prime Minister Metaxa and his definitive "no" (ohi) to an ultimatum made by Mussolini on October 28th 1940.

These are notes taken in my diary from the time when I was working there.

"There is excitement on the street in the village where I work as I arrive with friends to celebrate. The day is overcast but dry and the buildings take on a dreariness, blank -faced and featureless. Some large Greek flags hang limply on poles, as limp as the yellowing leaves which hang on the trees. Military music blares through loudspeakers on the street corner and the atmosphere swells with national pride. People assemble on both sides of the pavement waiting for the procession of local school children to start. The children march along the length of the street in their school uniforms carrying Greek flags and trying to look serious. I know nearly half the students in the procession, which is led by the youngest, trying not to stumble as they march with their flags. Some march engrossed in serious concentration: knees high, elbows beating back and fists punching the air as if they are extremely important. Others look around at the crowd, suppressing their excitement and stifling smiles. A few of them fail and wave to their parents and teachers with delight in their faces. The novelty of the march seems to have worn off for most of the older children who have performed it year after year. They go through the motions, but many look bored. Some even look a little self-conscious. Black and navy legs pass like a continuous wave. Slim long-legged girls all wearing black tights and short navy school skirts, the boys in navy trousers. I can tell which boys are going to be soldiers for some of them take the event extremely seriously, marching with precision and holding their flags high. When the procession has finished, the crowd are addressed through the loudspeaker and the national anthem is sung. They then disperse and my friends lead me off to a restaurant where we will have lunch."

Gold circles

While living in Greece I spent most of my weekends travelling to different parts of the country, visiting archaeological sites and museums, hiking on wild islands, visiting friends. One particular place which has always remained in my memory was the exhibition of the Royal Macedonian tombs at the museum of Thessaloniki.

The grave goods from these tombs are now housed in a state-of-the-art underground museum at the site of the tombs themselves, ancient Aigai, the equally ancient capital of Macedonia. It is now known as Vergina and is classified as a UNESCO world heritage site. The tomb complex was the burial place of Alexander the Great's father, of Philip II of Macedonia, and contained a wealth of gold, a true treasure trove of delight. At the time I was living in Greece, the museum at Vergina was not open as it is today.

The dark corridors of the Thessaloniki Museum were deliberately dimmed to show off the gold which radiated from well-lit glass display cabinets. I was blown away by the beauty and intricacy of the goldwork- the image of the 16- pointed sunburst, symbol of ancient Macedonia, which decorated the top of the ossuary which held Phillip II's bones and the image of which was repeated in the 8-pointed sun motifs which radiated from the top of caskets and decorated coins and golden discs. There were gold necklaces, gold diadems and other articles of jewellery, but it was the gold wreaths which really left a lasting impression.

Oak leaves and acorns had been fashioned in gold beaten so thin that the leaves looked lifelike and both they and the acorns looked as if they could have been plucked from the tree and dipped in liquid gold. However, they were all individually crafted from delicate sheets of gold and tied onto a gold ring using gold wire. The fecundity of leaves was impressive for they hung in huge clumps as if on a tree. The largest oak wreath was found in the Great tomb at Vergina, another smaller oak wreath was found in a tomb at nearby Derveni. Myrtle wreaths, equally delicate and dating, as the oak wreaths, to the 4th century BC were also on display.

There was something beautifully autumnal about the oak wreaths; leaves alongside acorns as they appear in this season. I always have assumed acorns to be poisonous but apparently, they were a staple in many ancient cultures. Ancient Greeks and Romans, of the lower echelons, ancient Japanese and American Indian relied on the abundance of acorns during a mast year to see them through the winter. Acorns spelled survival for these people. Perhaps this is partly why the oak was revered in so many ancient cultures-the ancient Greeks, Romans, Celts and Vikings to name but a few. Later in history, oak tannins were also used as dye and ink, ink was also made from the galls of the oak wasps, *Biorhiza pallida* (of the oak apple gall) and *Andricus kollari* (of the oak marble gall) which, although forming earlier in the year, are usually found large and round, the size of a marble on the backs of fallen oak leaves or on bits of branch in autumn.

Wreaths also hold significance. In ancient cultures they adorned the heads of significant people. Later, wreaths were used for superstitious purposes, crafted from dried grasses and hung on barn doorways to ensure a good harvest. Nowadays they are used on doorways as decoration. In Greece, doorways were traditionally hung with spring wreaths on May Day but in England I have noticed that autumn wreaths have become more popular in recent years. It is perhaps the abundance of leaves in beautiful colours which ask for them to be interwoven with crab apples, berries, dried grasses and dried flowers to make these decorative wreaths. My penchant for

Christmas-wreathed Georgian doorways with their strong symmetry, fanlights and ornate porches thus comes alive earlier in the year with the abundance of autumn wreaths hanging on these same doorways in local towns. The symmetry of the doorway itself is not the only pleasing feature, but also the symmetry of the circle.

The circle or ring is again an ancient symbol and a natural phenomenon. The cycle of the seasons as the earth orbits the sun (not purely circular in its orbit) the spherical planets, the spirals of galaxies, the appearance of the full moon as a disc when looked at from earth, likewise the setting sun, a solar eclipse when the circles of earth and sun superimpose in a near perfect fit which just gives a glimpse of a fiery flaming corona around the circumference of the circle. Then there are life cycles, the water cycle, the flow of blood around the body the sap moving around a tree, all of these cycles sustaining life. Although sap dies down in autumn, the tree stays alive.

Symbolically the circle is also known to represent an unbreakable bond as seen in the wedding ring, and from the Christian perspective a symbol of eternity through the cycle of birth, death, rebirth and resurrection to new life. It is a symbol of eternity, of hope and everlasting love. The circle is again the sacred choice of shape for Neolithic henges, the ring ditches around bronze age barrows. It has been said by some archaeologists that the circle of the henges represents the idea of a circular cosmos and the cycles of the moon and stars. There is so much mystery, so much left to learn and to understand. I like it this way for it fills the imagination with wonder.

I once bought my husband a telescope one Christmas, because I wanted to see the stars. I wanted to delve deeper into the universe, which is surely one of the deepest mysteries, and wondered if he would be interested too. There was nothing more wonderful and thrilling than seeing Saturn surrounded by its fragile ice rings catching the light of the sun in space, it completely blew my mind. So remote and ethereal was Saturn and its rings, even through a telescope, it was as if I were teetering on the edge of a beautiful dream, a world of not quite wakefulness, yet I knew that I was fully awake and what I was seeing was reality. I was on the outside looking in, looking into another world, the remote and icy world of Saturn shimmering and trembling, familiar from the pictures I had seen, yet somehow ghostly, unfamiliar, suspended in the dark depths of space. I felt this experience to be an immense privilege and perhaps shared some of the excitement that Galileo must have felt when he looked through the first telescope, extending his vision into a whole new cosmic realm and unlocking a whole new understanding. Such curiosity in those days nearly cost him his life, however.

Curiosity, the drive to a sense of discovery... this essence of humanity has never really changed, the wheel keeps turning, life continues but there is nothing really new under the sun. Despite science, we find the same inspiration and wonder in the same things as our ancestors did. Ancient people and scientists from the nearer future and today all obsessed with space. The night skies in Greece were indeed spectacular on dark remote island beaches away from bright lights and in lost lonely places, like the shadowy Cypriot olive grove which stood silently under the stars, only the warm breeze-breath riffling branches creating a soft sound. Here the stars stretched away with the ribbon of the milky way, remote and tantalising. Sometimes we could see satellites. I remember similar places in France where my father and I would also sit back and spot them, their orbits tracking across the night sky- slow moving stars. The Anthropocene has even changed the appearance of the night sky from earth such as we like to make our mark, our micro plastics left as a layer of sediment in the rocks for future generations to understand our reliance on artificiality. However, we still rely on the wheel, without which our modern world would not function. The wheel, a simple circle which is perhaps one of the most important innovations of all time, for it comprised the earliest form of technology and thus convenience. Although we might consider it mundane today, it has enabled humanity to progress through time and hence survive into the future.

Spain

Hiking with friends nearly every weekend in the Pyrenees while I lived in Spain, we would take tents or stay in abandoned shepherd's huts under the stars, away from the world. In autumn and winter these huts became quite cold and we would huddle around a fire in the evenings, not caring to get changed when we crept into our sleeping bags.

It was beautiful up there in autumn. In the Basque country especially, where we often went, the landscape seemed contained, Tolkienesque, quaint houses huddled on rugged, forested slopes, their glowing interiors and woodsmoke enticing as we wended our way on switchback roads through the dreamy dusk to our rather chilly accommodation. Small stone villages with hardly any inhabitants would always have a place of retreat, a rustic friendly restaurant where the locals (usually elderly) gathered to chat and we would arrive with our backpacks and dogs. The locals were always friendly and would give us a cordial welcome of jamon and cheese, crusty bread, soup, Spanish cerveza or deep red wine to while away the hours in comfort and glowing warmth while more often than not, the rain rang down on the wet cobbled streets outside and camping seemed to be off the agenda.

This was a far cry from the Basque country of France where I remember a summer as a teenager of 17 with my parents. We went to a classical music concert in a church in the quaint, fairytale town of St Jean de Luz where the evening was so hot that somebody in the audience fainted, and my father, a doctor, felt he had to go and attend, even though he spoke little French. I also remember the beach at Biarritz where the moon hung high on a warm sultry summer's night and I suddenly discovered that I was self-conscious about being with my parents and wanted only to be with the boy I had met at school, who I had just started seeing. An adventure which at that moment with my parents was frustratingly far beyond my reach.

But.... back to autumn in the Basque country with its colourful trees on forested slopes, its soft valleys and chattering streams. The cosy villages both there and in the Pyrenees, the mountain hamlets and abandoned villages with their quiet romanesque churches standing stoically in densely wooded valleys away from the world. These forests in autumn turn to gold, orange and life stands still just as it does in Greece and its rural villages where for those from the outside coming in, drawn like moths to a candle, the warmth of hospitality and community cordiality is abundantly shared.

France

Lyon, with its parks of yellowing leaves fading under a mist of mizzle. Here in the cosy autumn, we wander the city's shops and elegant cafes, visit picture-postcard stone villages which snuggle in its rural environs. Lyon sells itself as the gastronomic capital of France and the fish stuffed with walnuts does not disappoint. Walnuts are not the most obvious accompaniment to fish, but they bring out spectrum of subtle flavours giving the fish body and depth.

Deep in the Dordogne where honey-hued limestone exudes the richness of autumn there is a walnut mill. Golden is the oil which is squeezed from this precious crop, an oil flowing full of vitality and vitamin E. The mill is old, established, built of the same stone which comprises the crags of this rugged ancient landscape concealing caves where prehistoric people painted pictures of ancient animals, long since extinct, their existence forever time-trapped in mysterious shadowy recesses which never see the light of day.

We step into an organic interior of wood and stone, which seems to creak with centuries of use, living and breathing, infused with the sweet smell of sunlight and crushed shell where the walnuts have been broken, bruised by the great press. Sunlight slants across stone floors in large light patches. Inside is cool, contained, a dichotomous haven of peace and industry.

The walnut oil is beautiful on crusty bread or emulsified with fig or raspberry vinegar, mixed with a dash of French mustard and tossed on a salad, the same creamy dressing drizzled on steamed rainbow chard. It is sensational eaten with a soft creamy goat's cheese or blue cheese, accompanied by grapes, ripe pear and even runny honey and wild thyme. I love the mix of savoury and sweet.

Oil is seen as essential in this part of the world. Further south in the Mediterranean, a place of Roman ruins where the olives grow in groves which whisper silver and the autumn light lies calm and still in sun-soaked valleys, the olives yield their golden- green elixir. Olive oil is not only culinary but also medicinal and cosmetic. It is used as a base for many moisturising products and is also considered a healing balm, an anointing oil which holds spiritual associations in some religions. In addition, it is a source of light, no doubt used in Roman oil lamps, in Jewish menorah, where it was regarded as spiritual and eternal. It might have been even used to fuel the Olympic torch. Oil gives light and many small shrines in Greece are also filled with it. As an artist I use both olive oil and walnut oil to mix natural, powdered pigments into a paste, creating colours for sustainable paints.

The final product of the autumn bounty for which France is renowned is undoubtably its wine. Dreamy degustations in rolling vineyards where autumn still holds the heat of summer, and we are lost in its embrace beneath rustling golden leaves. We sip and savour rich reds with their mysterious melting chocolate or cherry, cassis tones and fresh whites with their citrusy carefree zest. Wine is the essence of France, and I still think they produce some of the best, although there are many other beautiful bottles to be savoured from other countries, my personal favourite being a sophisticated perfumed dry Muscat from Samos in Greece which brims with orange blossom.

Oil and wine, both bounties bottled, the sweet legacy of lazy summer sunshine encapsulated in the autumn harvest and guaranteed to make the winter better, rejuvenating body and soul.

SEA SKETCHES

Sand dollars

Back in England, Bournemouth, to be precise, waves roll rhythmically with a reassurance which is calming as I wander the shoreline, sand soft underfoot, strewn with shells and other sea debris. I am not planning to pay any attention today to what the sea has left lying about; my intention is to walk, to make it to a far-flung groyne in the half an hour that I have left of my lunchbreak from work. I am stopped in my tracks. Scattered about like the beads from a bracelet are small white discs each pierced with a small central hole. "Plastic waste?" I wonder "somebody's bracelet broke and the beads spilled like seashells on the shore." I stop to pick one up, the underside is etched with a tiny star. I hold a tiny urchin on my hand, an organism of such symmetrical perfection and beauty, a design which delights the heart and excites the eyes. I pick another and another; small, they slip into my pocket; I assume they are sand dollars, I have never seen such treasure on the beach before, never knew they even existed in the UK. They seem to me more valuable than money as I move slowly along the shoreline, seeing them at every step, some only a few millimetres across, others slightly larger. I take a few more, a delicious sense of satisfaction mingled with the wonder as when one sees a snow-flake. There is something about stars. If I am not careful, I will have a pocket full of sand dollars. That would be greedy. I must leave them alone for other beachcombers to become equally excited, or for the turn of the tide to take them away.

Yet I cannot stop looking, peering among the shells in their array of shapes and colours; equally beautiful. Salmon pink cockles lie beside slipper limpets and crab's claws, tellins of all colour combinations-grey and white, pink and ochre, beige and brown. They shine in the sun while still wet, basking in brilliance. But it is the sand dollars which are to be my bounty, and I wonder where they came from and why they are here, lying in the sand; treasures which I have had the fortune to discover.

Once home, I enquire of Dr Google, iden-tifying them as pea urchins (*Echinocyamus pusillus*); tiny sea urchins which live a soli-tary life on the seabed around the British coast. These are the empty casts, bleached by the sun, the bodies having died, the spines shed. I wonder what caused them to die in such abundance and why so many came to be washed up here upon Bournemouth beach. I think of them being separated from their dark and mysterious world under the sand, flung into the brilliance above the waves through which the surfers ride with glistening spume and the gulls call and swoop.

Perhaps their death was due to temperatures being higher on into autumn this year - it is mid-October and still nearly 20 degrees today. This is the only explanation I can come up with, but I am not a scientist and no one else has commented on them on the internet, perhaps they have not looked or seen.

The pea urchins remain present on the beach for the rest of the week and on into the next, although their numbers diminish as every evening the sea takes some of them back to itself, to be reclaimed by the waves. A few stay surrendered to the softer sand further away from the shoreline, where they have probably been swept by the incoming tide. After two weeks, all trace of them has gone and beachcombing resumes normality but always tinted with wonder and surprise.

Since that time, I have never found them in such abundance, I have also realised since they are best found here in autumn. I have hardly seen them in spring or summer, apart from the odd stray, and also not many in winter. It is perhaps to do with tide or current here in Bournemouth, or whether it is breeding season, and the sea temperature causes them to come ashore. I profess to having no knowledge and am merely hypothesising about this fact on which Dr Google remains silent.

There is something so exciting in the process of collecting, of assembling the shells and sea urchins that I have taken and putting them in a small jar, of looking at their range of autumnal colours; the browns, russets, pinks and purples, creams and greys and thinking back to the beach and the multifariousness of structure and form, the blends of colour, texture and pattern, these small and simple wonders which make the world so diverse, rich, abundant. These are the testimonies to other worlds within our own, of organisms which we know so little about. These are the creatures which make their bed the seabed, carrying out their dark days away from the familiar world which we inhabit, in a mysterious and compelling watery world beneath the waves.

As a child I had a lamp made of seashells, the empty test of a large sea urchin being the lampshade through which the bulb softly and comfortably glowed. In that shop in Cornwall, I begged my parents to purchase one, a purple urchin on a pedestal decorated with scallops and other smaller seashells. To me it was something liberating, reassuring and soothing, shaping beautiful dreams and taking my mind freely into the mystery and imagination of the deep and to the secret lives of creatures beneath the sea.

Provenance and destiny

The sand is soft under foot, the shoreline dreamy, whimsical; woven with ribbons of seaweed which wend their way, stretching along the shoreline. On the horizon rises the Isle of Wight, its needles bright in the sunlight. To the left lies the hump of Hengistbury Head, gilded by the sunshine. Once situated inland on the river Solent, when the sea stood beyond the chalk ridge, of which remains only the needles to the East and Old Harry Rocks to the west, Hengistbury has been inhabited for in excess of 10,000 years. As well as being a site for a bronze age cemetery it became, latterly, a strategic location with defensive ditches and a very important seaport, both in the Iron Age and during the times of the

Romans. Now abandoned to the elements, this ancient port is a site of special scientific interest and supports a wealth of wildlife. I imagine ships containing exotic cargo from other parts of the world docking there, the colourful clamour, the cacophony of sounds and scents, a hub of humanity now silenced.

At Bournemouth the beach is also out-of-season silent, and the sea has carried its own cargo to be abandoned here. One such treasure is undoubtedly a piece of smooth sea glass, its curves caressed by the waves. I love finding sea glass; its pale green or aqua hues reflecting the delicate wash of the sea on a warm autumn day such as this one. Once sand itself, glass is a product of transformation, of metamorphosis, of sand being extensively heated, melted and rapidly cooled. It therefore becomes a new structure in itself. There is nothing new in glassmaking, and I finger the pendant made of Roman glass which I wear around my neck. The Romans were great glass makers, producing exquisite, beaded jewellery as well as receptacles such as delicate jugs, perfume bottles and bowls. I imagine such beautiful glassware might well have been amongst the cargo on the Roman ships which docked at Hengistbury Head. But before the Romans, the ancient Egyptians also made glass, regarding it as precious. It is interesting that such a commodity is now regarded as something so cheap and throwaway that we find it washed up on the shore, returning to the sand from where it first came.

Time is the essence of smooth sea glass. It can take anything from between five and thirty years being tumbled by the waves, the result of movement and friction, wind and wave, sand and salt. There is something beautifully elemental about this process of change, and also something so marvellous that a material as fragile and breakable as glass can be transformed, strengthened by the elements, the whims of the waves, to be at the mercy of tide and time. It speaks of change, just as autumn is a season of change, and that we can also be strengthened and transformed through life changes.

I find glass in different stages of transformation. Some is still sharp and essentially brittle, some slightly softened with the beginnings of a frosty formation spreading across its surface. Some is thicker, some thinner. The more frosted and smoother-sided the older, rather than being weather-worn, beaten and battered, chips and knocks are essentially smoothed. Are we smoothed by life's knocks? Are our chips worn away as we become older and less worried about what others think? I like to think so. Even though outwardly we do not wear as well as the glass, our smooth soft youthful complexions taking on a more expressive and wrinkled hue, which I like to see as laughter lines and the outward evidence of experience, inwardly perhaps we are softened yet strengthened through experience too.

The destiny of the sea glass that I pick up is varied. Much of it will go into artwork, some will sit in cosy glass jars around my house with pieces of driftwood and shells, all having been brought in on a wild tide and salvaged; all, as the evenings draw in darker, contained from the outside world and illuminated by little lights. The pieces which I don't pick up might be made into jewellery by local artisans who fashion silver and sea glass earrings and pendants of pure delight.

I wonder at the provenance of this glass as I roll a piece around in my palm, its texture salty smooth, not shiny smooth, all sharp edges softened and subdued, a hard soft-ness fashioned by the sea. I wonder from where and how far it came to be washed up on Bournemouth beach. The colour of this particular piece is more unusual, a sort of leaf green, as the majority I find is either aqua marine or clear. I imagine this was once a wine bottle, perhaps coming from nearby France, a small step across the channel. I am not an expert on tides and the way the waves might wash around the coast but as the channel is a small corridor between England and France, I would imagine that things could get carried easily from coast to coast and it would be harder for things to travel from say, the North Sea or the Atlantic to the thin strip which is the Channel, that is not to say that they do not though.

If this bottle came from France, it could have been filled with wine from a sunny French vineyard, a crisp dry white, as red is not usually kept in green glass bottles. The thought of it conjures pictures of lazy autumn evenings, the setting of the sun slanting between the crimson leaves of rustling vines, layers of last light reaching out to touch the hillsides and fuse the land-scape with fingers of gold before falling away to be drenched in dusk. The wine could have been consumed in a French restaurant, the long lingering looks of lovers across a wooden table, candlelight

and the cosy chill of autumn evenings, inti-
macy intensified by the easy flow of wine.

My imagination is running away with
me. I will never know the provenance of
this piece of glass and how long it has been
abandoned to the sea. But now it has found
a new destiny. It is like the small piece of
pottery that I found in a forest recently
while walking beneath trees which flamed
with the fires of autumn colours. The small
shard was decorated with a blue and white
diamond motif. I am not a pottery expert
by any means, and without a hallmark
or a knowledge of patterns representing
certain times or places, it is impossible to
know where it might have been made or
when. But I sensed it was something old as
slight irregularity in the pattern suggested
it to be hand painted, not printed, the glaze
not shiny, the pottery thick ceramic, not
delicate porcelain. Perhaps it was a piece
of plate from a Victorian or an even earlier
table. I wonder who once ate off it and how
the plate was broken and discarded. Was
it thrown in a fit of rage during a domestic?
Accidentally dropped? I will never know
but what fascinates me more is how
these curios stimulate curiosity, and how
one can weave a whole web of fantasy
around such a fragment. It is like the small

stone which I found in some gravel in the grounds of a local museum. Someone had once inscribed a heart on it in black ink. There it was lying in the gravel, waiting to be found. Why had someone done that? Whatever its provenance I pocketed it, to give it a new destiny.

Back to the sea glass which presents itself in varied stages of shape and form, of smoothness, size and colour (normally clear or aqua marine, sometimes different shades of green. Beer bottle brown is elusive, and I have yet to find royal blue or amber). It is a wonder washed up on the tide, for the piece which I hold in my hand is testimony to a story secret to itself. A new story can be conjured with the imagination, but the old story is lost to tide and time.

Roses

Roses can be grown in any season. With flowers imported from hotter climes, grown under glass and polytunnels in the depths of winter, like fruit out of season, they are available all year round. With climate change it is even true to say that roses can still flower in December in southern England some years and certainly in autumn. Fuchsias, roses and many other flowers continue to thrive even after the first frost and certainly into December in my garden. So, I am not unduly surprised to see three red roses strewn across the sand on Bournemouth beach in autumn. What is more intriguing is their story.

They are not placed on the sand in a special location, as if to carefully commemorate someone's passing, but they are squashed into it, right in the middle of the beach amidst all the pugmarks and footprints of passersby, people probably stepping on them unwittingly as they lie there subdued and submerged in sand. The flowerheads are not fully open yet, a promise of hope and a future of florescence crushed, suffocated by sand. Bruised and trampled, these buds, prevented from fulfilling their promise and potential, seem to symbolise the pain of a broken heart, and with it, shattered dreams. Were they given by a secret admirer and deliberately rejected by the admired? Were they cast away after a bitter breakup of two lovers? Or even a man and wife? A wedding anniversary gone sour, an argument here on the sand? Or perhaps they were simply blown out of a bouquet, offered as a memorial to someone passed. I will never know, but to me the budding roses are like the young adolescent love we all experienced in our teens with words which at the time bore so much beauty, held so much hope and promise, words which hung on the heart and meant so much until everything became nothing and the words unravelled; becoming fragmented phrases, empty of meaning, blown away on the wind like rose petals or like the last leaves of autumn.

I like the idea that everything that is spoken can never be unsaid because the sounds and syllables of those words travel on through time and space. But surely space doesn't echo with the cacophony of all that has ever been spoken as those soundwaves travel further and further away from their source. Yet it is an interesting thought, and one which comforts, for those words which once spoke so much promise could never be undone, echoing in the higher echelons of the universe, never finding a destination, resonating in space for all time, even though time in space perhaps does not exist. Therefore, we should be careful what we say for, if this is true, the hurtful things as well as the good, can also last forever.

This is a similar idea as to what happens to thoughts and cares cast into the sea. A hastily scribbled message stuffed into a bottle and thrown away, a bottle sealed like lips until it is opened, its secrets spilled. Words will often survive the stormy seas for generations, staying silent through time, the years of being bottled up. Someone else other than the intended recipient will read them, but they are never left unspoken, can never be unsaid.

Time is a great healer and some life changes, which might seem to break us at the time, can serve to strengthen us. So as we undergo sea glass like transformation, a broken bottle being buffeted by the rollercoaster waves of life, taking the ups and downs, the rough with the smooth, we can learn to ride the storms like the bottle, and like the seaglass, hope to come out stronger on the incoming tide.

Ancient isle

It is obviously autumn, although one would not know it on a beach necessarily. As I continue to scour the shoreline, I find a few stray autumn leaves— oak leaves crumpled brown, a small silver birch leaf turned yellow, a crimson maple leaf and another as bright as a flame. These are all cast aside along with the spiky case of a sweet chestnut and a couple of large hazelnuts. I wonder where they came from and how they got here.

Out across the water rises the chalk headland of the Isle of Wight, the iconic needles, a mirage trembling, scintillating suspense. I have always been intrigued by the Isle of Wight ever since I discovered its coloured sands as a child and learned that you could find fossils in many of its secret coves. But the most exciting discovery was surely the ancient causeway found beneath the Solent. As I already alluded, 8000 years ago, the Isle of Wight was attached to the mainland. The English Channel is thought to have been created when sea levels rose at the end of the Ice Age, separating Britain, which was once a peninsular of northern Europe, from France. Excavations in the Solent using core soil samples have revealed evidence of grain, twigs, leaves and other organic materials. But it was the ancient causeway which really fired my imagination. The perfect preservation of something prehistoric, the black bedraggled wood fitting together like a complex jigsaw puzzle when the archaeologists reassembled it. This causeway was a feat of engineering connecting communities and surviving the test of time. It shows, as does the port at Hengistbury Head, how sophisticated prehistoric people actually were, how they built networks and traded, communicated and constructed.

The wood of the causeway was not the only organic matter to survive. Archaeologists also found 8,000-year-old oak leaves preserved in the mud. I consider this to be truly awesome in the overwhelming sense of the word. The sea here seems so permanent as it washes in and out as regular as the systolic and diastolic beats of the heart. It is a sound echoed through the ages, but from the not so remote recesses of ancient time.

The presence of discarded hazelnuts on Bournemouth beach for me triggers an association with the Isle of Wight for it was also revealed on a documentary (it could even have been the same one) that the Solent submerged low-lying forests, obviously of oak but also hazel, and that semi fossilised hazelnuts, affectionately known as "Noah's nuts" from this time are sometimes exposed in the eroded sediment at Compton Bay on the Isle of Wight. It would seem that 8,000 years ago the ubiquitous hazel tree which pops a brilliant yellow display along so many leafy lanes in the gloom of autumn and provides a nut with a warmth of flavour, was also welcomed by ancient foragers just as it has been by those going nutting all through the centuries. Hazelnuts are traditionally ready to harvest in September, the beginning of autumn, as are most nuts. An autumn staple full of energy and protein, one that keeps and can be stored for when the winter bites. I pick up one of the hazelnuts from the beach, holding it in my hand, and wonder at this tiny form which can sustain and provide, a tiny-packed punch of energy and nutrition which can transform into a tree and holds so much promise and hope by containing all the DNA it needs to sustain this miracle of metamorphosis. Again, I am awe-inspired. Life is full of small miracles if we think about them, and we can find them everywhere if we look for them.

Metal

The man with the metal detector moves slowly across the sand, headphones on, a clean swinging sweep of the arm, head down, utterly absorbed. I wonder what he will find beneath the sand apart from the odd coin, ring pull or crunched up can. Someone once found a wedding ring, I believe. Its story excites the imagination. Was it flung off deliberately during a row, a final fling symbolising separation from a marriage which wasn't working? Did it belong to a broken heart or one which had found another? the thin gold band, the circle of eternity proving untruthful. Perhaps it belonged to a love still cherished, the ring lost while swimming in the sea. How old was this ring and from which country did if come? Endless questions left unanswered, stories, secrets buried in the sand.

Despite such tantalising yet hopefully rare finds as this, I am sure metal detecting must be more fulfilling in the countryside, especially if you are looking for archaeological finds. It is something I have always wanted to have, a metal detector, as an archaeology enthusiast, it seems to be the next most logical thing to digging. But with limited free time, I have shelved the idea so far. People out in the fields armed with metal detectors have unearthed no end of fascinating discoveries; hordes of Roman coins, bronze age weaponry, Roman buckles and belts to name but a few things I remember from documentaries on television. But it is not the value of what is found, it is the fact that something is ancient and can help to transform our knowledge of life in the past.

Very occasionally the most surprising

archaeological things can even be found on the beach, and without the aid of a metal detector, like the little boy, aged 6, from Sussex who picked up a rather "strange rock" which turned out to be a neanderthal hand axe. During the autumn of 2024 as I write this book, archaeologists have been analysing it and have come to the conclusion that it must have been buried on the seabed, perhaps in an area which used to be land, such as the Solent. Of course, being Sussex, it would perhaps not have come from the Solent, but maybe from an ancient riverbed in the English Channel or Doggerland, the mysterious land which once connected Britain to northern Europe and which is now submerged by the North Sea. It is hypothesis and speculation, we will never know its story, its provenance. We can only wonder at who fashioned it and what it was used for and how it ended up on a beach in Sussex for a little boy to find. If the child had not been curious enough to pick it up and take it home it would, like the many fossils which go unfound, have been returned to the tide and lost forever.

Sand speak

The sand also tells stories if you can

decipher them and today is no exception. A wide expanse of mirror wash reflects the clouds on this radiant day, the kind of day when it really feels that it is good to be alive. Rill marks score the sand, wandering in angular furrows down towards the sea where more sand is sculpted into small cushions, the deep ridges of a fish-scaled back, a mackerel sky. Light flows above their rounded forms, glistening gold in trembling pools of stranded seawater which mirror more clouds. It is a phenomenon of weather, wind and tide coming together in a combination which creates this special effect.

Someone has scrawled in the sand a message, drawn a heart. Another has built a castle, left to ruin. A dog has perhaps precipitated this process for pug marks pass near it and beyond. The sand is pitted with the pugmarks of playful dogs, now it is autumn, and they are allowed back onto the beach. They are accompanied by human footprints, mostly clad, not the bare, carefree footprints of summer.

After a storm, the strandline is strewn with seaweed and slipper limpets. They lie encrusted in sand, half buried by the blast of the wind and the pounding rain which occurred earlier. Usually, I do not find much rubbish, for Bournemouth beach is regularly cleaned by litter pickers who set about their task early. One autumn day, however, after a storm, I find a plastic penguin, rotund, robust, and evidently not the worst for wear for bobbing about in the sea. Plastic is indestructible so it would seem. There is also a small doll, her blond nylon hair full of sand, her unblinking eyes staring into the sky, a frozen smile. Each, no doubt, has its own story attached, if it could talk. How long had they been out at sea? Where had they come from? Who had they belonged to? The nurdles too, in abundance. Pieces of plastic looking like fish eggs, manufactured to be melted down to make more items of plastic. Pernicious along all our coasts, I wonder if they have escaped from ships which have accidently released their cargo into the sea. How else do they enter our oceans? I would love to know their story so that they could be stopped.

One of my friends saw some flowers on the beach, early one autumn morning when the sea was gentle, milky calm infusing with the misty horizon, the air crisp so that breath curled on the gleaming golden air and the sun touched the sand with long luminescent fingers. From the photos which he sent me on Whatsapp, the sea was shining like crystal that hopeful morning, his paddleboard primed. It wasn't just flowers which my friend saw, but petals cast before the waves near a small dressed up doll in traditional clothes. We wondered if it was part of some sort of ceremony, a religious ritual. We will never know the story, but Bournemouth is quite cosmopolitan.

Back on my beach this day, gull footprints walk whimsical paths, straight lines converging and doubling back, crisscrossing the higher sand. In one place a patch of them suggests a confrontation, the tell-tale sand is churned, ridged with many feet, the three toed claws superimposed on themselves, the sand scratched and scraped leaving the legacy of action, most probably a meal they were bickering over as gulls do.

Further along, the sand has been sculpted by a cross wind, higher up the beach it leaves a residue of wavy patterns again superimposed in complex ridged layers streaked with shells; each shell a comet leaving a trail, especially down by the water's edge where every tail points away from the sea and each nucleus seems to be drawn to it as if trying to return to the deep.

The beach is a mystery, known only unto itself. The washed-up shells, each a life which once was. Some are still alive. A crow takes a shell in its beak and flying high, drops it onto the promenade. It repeats the action several times until satisfied that the shell is broken enough that it can be prised apart and the contents devoured. Such intelligence.

My shoes are full of sand, and there is always some sand and a shell or two in the pockets of every coat I possess. Sand gets everywhere, between the teeth, in the ears; it is gritty, and sometimes annoying but it is wonderful, and I wouldn't want it any other way. When looked at through a microscope, each grain reveals a complexity of shapes and wonderous forms. Small stars vie with shiny cylinders, some forms are long like rice grains, different colours, patterns, microscopic pieces of stone, shell and marine life each imprinted with a unique pattern. It blows my mind. The sand tells a story in itself, through its composition, the ground down debris of centuries, soft and smooth enough to sink into, yet gritty and grainy when inside something. A grain of sand moves with the tide, taking its zigzag course around the coast, or blown in the wind to travel further. Groynes along the beach, ugly yet necessary, stop it in its tracks. Otherwise, the beautiful beach at Bournemouth would not retain its blue flag award for there would be no sand to indulge in, to tell us stories.

Streams of consciousness

Today the sand is scoured and swept clean, washed by the waves, the froth and foam. Strings of seaweed leave their line along the shore, whips of weed with long, languorous fronds twisted around on themselves like letters telling an indecipherable story, bladderwrack wrapped alongside. There are hardly any shells; only a lump of driftwood discarded by the sea, old and tired as the year which is winding down. The sand dollars have disappeared.

As I stare out to sea, its colours seem to thread like skeins of silk in the movement of the waves: vitreous bottle green, aqua marine and blue; or they appear so to my eyes. My photos show something different and I realise that we often live in an illusion, the way we interpret things and see things can be different from the way someone else sees them; literally, physically. I am talking about colours, perspectives, not thoughts or perceptions. And as I look, I realise that I am literally seeing through tinted glasses a deeper intensity, a subtle spectrum of blue which my cheap camera cannot capture, and when my glasses come off, neither can my eyes. What we see is so often altered, filtered, manipulated, changed, so that we are made to see it in a different way from reality. Even the autumn colours look less intense without sunglasses to filter their fragmented light. Yet life, or various aspects of it, can be a beautiful illusion which we can step into and embrace.

Time told in a shell

A wild and windswept sea as wind whips the waves into a frenzy. They ride to the shore constantly coming in, like horses with manes streaming. I am alone on the beach, following a path where whispers of sand wander along the stretch of shoreline and then break into a run, fleeting phantoms chasing across the sand's smooth surface. The roar of waves echoes in the empty expanse where I walk alone, feeling the awe of the atmosphere, the strength and security of the sea, a permanent presence. There is little to find today, save a few strands of seaweed and then I spy a shell-large and grey with rich russet-coloured ridges turning to amber like the leaves of autumn. I am told that if you count the bands of a shell, you will discover its age. This shell is large; bigger than my hand, with deep horizontal ridges and a contour like the crest of a wave. Its numerous tightly knit horizontal bands of amber, verdigris, copper-brown and charcoal black would probably make it at least a century old, although they are too diffi-cult to count.

I think of this shell; alive during the whole of my life, of my parent's lives, born perhaps when my grandparents were born or even before. I wonder how it survived in the sea with so many pred-ators and what sort of life it led. It is hard to understand what a shell experiences, or rather the creature living within it, something so alien to our own existence. Yet I find anything so different from us to be fascinatingly mysterious and I want to know more about its world. I think of this shell just as I thought about the sand dollars living out their lives on the dark seabed away from the world. Being wrenched away by the waves and depos-ited on the shore is surely to be thrust into an anathema, a nightmare perhaps to one which seeks such a subdued and solitary existence on the ocean floor. For us, an equivalent might be being born, ejected from our watery world into a brave new existence. Perhaps because of this trauma, none of us have any conscious memories of our birth.

Robin conversation

The strip of sand is almost under water at Shipstal's secluded beach where cliffs tumble down to the sand and roots reach into the sea when the tide is high. On a balmy gentle autumn day, it is almost tropical. The sea laps, licking the sand with wavelets and tongues of weed. Today there is no curlew's bubbling call but rather a cadence of cadenzas as a robin sings lustily, its jingling silver penny tones bright in the autumn sunshine while another answers from a nearby rowan tree studded with scarlet berries.

The robin sings then listens again, its head cocked on one side, bright eyes beady and expectant, holding hope. Its friend replies, a babbling conversation sweeter than any music and lyrical against the lap of the sea. They hold my attention for many minutes, the pair just conversing together, a sound sweet, exuberant ringing out to sea, regardless of who is listening.

Leaves and birds

I love to walk beneath the trail of Aspen trees which leads along to the hide, listening to the empowering psithurism of their golden leaves. The wind surges then drops, the trees responding, as if echoing the atmosphere.

In the hide all is quiet and still. I could sit for hours just watching, waiting. It is my favourite place to be and on a gin clear day of liquid calm one can see quite clearly. I have watched many a migrant bird over the autumn and winter months. Most spectacular for me are the avocets with their delicate daintiness. I have watched them coming across the vast expanse of wash, a flowing form of unity, silver shot with shadows as the birds change course in one soft sweep. There is such synchrony to their flight, like starlings mumurating, that the whole spectacle is astonishing. Today, there is no such spectacle, but a cormorant sits astride a post, huge rubbery feet dripping down over it. It stands posed, poised, waiting for something and nothing in true cormorant fashion.

Wandering back past birch forests where sunlight torches the tree trunks and the breeze surges, stirring their delicate heads to toss with cascading golden fountains. Silver darts shoot amidst shifting shadows, leaves riffle, everything echoes energy and the delicious delirium of dancing light in this carefree, fairytale forest beneath a blaze of blue.

The heather has fast faded, subdued purple pockets blend into an autumn background and the blaze of blue sea beyond. Berries stab the scene with colour – rosehips, holly, guelder rose and hawthorn. A doe roams quietly in the thicket, so silently that one feels her presence long before one sees her eyes staring. Once seen, she bounds away, bob-tail retreating into the trees.

It is still early autumn, and the sun is still strong. Dragon-flies dart above the lakes and mate on solid surfaces; their red bodies resemble the rosehips mentioned before. All seems colour coordinated. The robin's red breast as he sits and sings from a holly bush and the red admiral's wings completing the colour wheel. I savour it, for autumn's initial blaze of glory will soon be gone.

Back on the beach at Bournemouth...

Back on the beach at Bournemouth where we are in the grip of an Indian summer, the seaweed strewn tideline is cluttered with cuttlefish bones and a litter of leaves- oak and horse chestnut; brown and abandoned on the shore. A few hazel-nuts again add to the mix, and I wonder where they came from. Despite being the end of October, I walk in short sleeves, my coat slung over my shoulder, my phone reading 20 degrees. People paddle and swim in the sea in swimsuits, many on the beach are still in shorts.

It is definitely warmer now than it was when I was a child. In those days, I would stand outside on bonfire night while my feet froze in large throbbing lumps and I couldn't move my toes, or my fingers either for that matter. This is comfortable, but it's strange. Autumns and winters have been so much warmer over the past decade that without the autumn colours to give us the hint, it would be hard to discern the seasons at all. If I close my eyes and feel the sun still strong on my skin and the caress of calm, warm wind coming in off the sea, it could still be summer.

Catharsis

As I walk by the sea today, I am driven by

its sense of calm, the placid wash, gentle, comforting. It is what I need to overcome the pain of missing. As I am drawn deep into this delicious, embalming atmosphere, soothed, enriched, my imagination begins to wander away from myself and out into the sea, as if the waves were a refuge, the mysterious deep, home to many weird and wonderful creatures. In that space where I felt freedom and happiness, I now feel the ache of absence, of treasured times passed, and yet the waves wash in gently, consoling, as if to say time goes on in continuum but the past can be present if you want it to stay.

Others would not find nearly as much consolation from the sea. Those who have lost loved ones to the deep. Only last year two teenagers drowned here and an acquaintance of mine also fell to his death in the depths further around the coast. A bittersweet sea, depending on what associations you hold. For the tourist fun and freedom, for those who lost loved ones, a place of sadness and remorse. The weather can also change the mood. As today it is gentle, teasing out tender emotions and soothing the soul, tomorrow it might be stormy, the venting of passions.

I have been intrigued by atmosphere ever

since I was a child, being caught up in the feeling of a place. I have always wondered what causes atmosphere and am very sensitive to it. My mother told me back then that it was the feeling left behind in a place, memories of people past. I certainly loved the sense of history, the feeling of a forgotten past when I went into old buildings, but it can not be entirely true that memories of the past infuse the present because in every place, different people have experienced either happiness or sadness in equal measure, have different memories and varying perceptions of a place through their experience of it. One of my favourite rooms in the National Trust property where I volunteer, for example, is to me peaceful and restful and yet someone once died in that room and so it was perhaps a place of sadness for some.

I am now beginning to wonder if it is our own perception of a place, coupled with the way we are feeling at the time, who we are with, the associations a place brings about in our mind's eye and physical aspects such as weather, which conjures a sense of atmosphere unique to us. Like looking through tinted lenses, our judgements are maybe coloured by all these things and most of all by imagination, linked to our own knowledge and experience which influences the way a place feels. I really don't know if this is true and whether others are experiencing the same atmosphere as I am experiencing at the same place in the same moment in time.

It is as when one looks at a painting and sees something different from somebody else. For every picture perhaps tells a unique story to its viewer as every piece of music touches the heart differently and draws a range of emotions and associations. Perhaps atmosphere is the same to some extent, or maybe it is more complex. It still intrigues me that despite what went on in a place, some seem essentially carefree, some deeply tragic, others historic, some overwhelmingly peaceful, and some troubled and melancholy to the majority of people who experience them. I do not know how much of atmosphere is real and how much is an illusion or a perception, but all I know is its ability for it to draw us into itself so that we become hopelessly lost in it and totally inspired and fascinated by it. That is the way it has always affected and enthralled me so that I hold an endless fascination for it, for through it I hold a connection with place, as if the place seems to speak and feel, even though it is unfeeling and inanimate, and I can respond to it.

Storms

When storms sweep the shores late autumn and on throughout the winter, I feel a fragile sense of excitement stirring. Watching the waves; their colours churning in shades of marl, grey and steely blue, wind buffeting the sand, whipping and whistling between the beach huts. On some beaches, waves crash against the harbour wall, sending up spray and spume meters high, only to come crashing down with stupendous force which sets the excitement up a gear.

I have just read a book about coastal erosion; specifically about the north coast of Norfolk where my brother and I used to holiday as children with our parents and delinquent dog. How could I forget the freezing North Sea, where I was taught to swim and out of which I would emerge, shivering in summer. The long beaches on the north Norfolk coast provided endless excitement and discovery and I would pick up carnelians by the handful. The cliffs were picturesque and statuesque, and I loved to find features in their contours, the collision and contortion of colours found in their eroding faces. In Norfolk it was always windy, and we would erect the windbreak on our little patch of sand where it would buzz furiously whenever the wind tugged at its stretched canvas frame. Flags flapped frantically by the café, where we might buy ice cream, the wind making sure it would add sand to our sweet treat as well as to our eyes, but it didn't dampen our spirits. It was in Norfolk that my brother and I went shrimping with plastic nets and helped our father build supersized sand-castles on the shoreline; proper fortresses with moat, bailey and turrets galore. Just as wind and wave washed away these castles, so it seems it is doing the same to the Norfolk coast.

Coastal erosion occurs naturally causing the coastline to change subtly through time. As the cliffs retreat, their edges coming closer to civilisation, so entire villages with churches and cottages have been claimed through the centuries by the sea. The land on which they stood, exists no more than as a pile of rubble down on the beach which will eventually be washed away forever by the waves. All that remains are faded photographs and the memories of the people who farmed and lived on the land which is no longer. I marvel at how something so solid as a cliff can actually be so transitory, but then nothing physical lasts forever, however strong. It makes one understand and appreciate the vulnerability of life and the earth on which it lives.

Although coastal erosion is natural, it has been exacerbated in recent years by a profundity of storms, or so the scientists say. The frequency and severity of storms are accelerating the erosion process. This is obviously of concern for people who live on the cliff top, for people whose roots and livelihoods are there, but it should be of concern for all of us. Yet every cloud has a silver lining and for archaeologists, geologists and historians, the prospect of erosion is the revealing and exposing of new secrets and wonders. For fossil hunters, the autumn and winter with their frequent storms, is prime time for scouring the shoreline of the Jurassic coast, near to where I live, in order to see what new novelties have been revealed by the eroding cliffs.

My fascination with fossils ensures that I will take any opportunity to hunt for them, keeping an open eye and an open mind in nearly every location. As well as finding fossils in fields and in forests, I have found them up mountains, on Greek islands and in gravel driveways, as well as in the more obvious places. It was one autumn I went to Chapman's pool on the Jurassic coast once the tourists had gone and the place was alone. It is not classed as a fossil hotspot, but the imprints of ammonites in the brittle shale are everywhere evident. A scramble down from the coast path along a thin track which weaves down through the debris of old landslips now thick with bramble, rosehip and old man's beard, takes us to the cove. We stumble out onto the shoreline. From above, the cove is a perfect semi-circle, an amphitheatre cut by the spill of the sea which washes in like a calming breath and leaves the zigzag of a corona as it washes out.

On the beach, the corona and the curve of the cove is too large to perceive from the inside, a bit like the circle of the earth being undiscernible from earth itself, but this inability to perceive somehow helps to augment the awesome expanse of silence. A wan sun streaks the sky and licks the water with a pearly hue. Cold bites at fingers and face while the waves wash in and leave with a hiss of undertow.

The swallows have long gone, I watched them back in summer flitting over the sea jabbing the air with their tiny piercing cries. The only signs of life now are the washed up cuttle fish bones on the beach, and the rock pipits which scurry around looking for food. Elemental; light, rock, water and air: this place exists by itself, for itself creating its own benevolence, the wind stirring the ghosts of memories which walk here on the beach, giving it its presence and purpose. This is a hard place which doesn't care, and yet it seems to encircle everything in its embrace.

We are the only two people here, my husband and I. Alone with the wave's wash and contained in the cove's calm serenity. It is as if it were a secret we had just discovered because we were the only ones watching, stumbling upon this ancient amphitheatre on whose stage something similar has been played out since the dawn of time. There would obviously be changes to the stage set; erosion continues to change and shape the coastline, and it is impossible to know how long this cove has existed. Yet the rocks with all their striped sediment, everything in this environment tells a story, an open history book inviting us to step inside. The fossils are just a fragment of that time's continuum, an ancient time represented in their strange spirals and whorls. We stand at the other edge of time, out on the shoreline where the sea washes in constantly, subtly changing, and revealing new treasures and secrets which can be collected in our consciousness.

Heavy weather

I wanted to see the sea like this, so I took my chance with the gap in the clouds, a chink in the steely grey armour of the sky. I went on foot, which was a mistake because by the time I got to the beach, the heavens opened. That window of opportunity for the sun to shine had been barely 15 minutes before the rain returned with a vengeance- soaking and spitting strong projectiles.

But my mind was set on experiencing the elements, sharing something of the scene. There is something deliciously dreamy and cosy about a British beach when it is storm swept, windswept; a bedraggled beach where all the strong storm colours wash into each other with an augmented whisper. Diminished light, blurring mist and moist; only a glimmer of hope behind Old Harry. The tide was out, and the waves raced in; roaring, rushing with such speed but no great height. Exhilarating.

Windswept and soaked- what a way to go back to work!! But this is what I had half expected, to experience the storm. I needed to be at one with the world which I so often paint, to feel the raw autumnal elements blasting my face, tugging my hair. I am exhausted with the artificial office atmosphere, its disconnection with the outside world, observations only made through glass. On the inside looking out.

I was almost alone on the abandoned beach. Only a very few reckless sea spectators like me were enjoying the storm. Everyone else was sensibly heading for some shelter somewhere or had not ventured out at all. One man with a child on his shoulders stood looking at the waves, a couple turned about and headed back, a group of girls left the sand. I stood alone, soaked, looking out to sea, at the swell, the roar, the whip of the waves and felt such excitement and freedom at the big blank canvas of this beach with its unframed horizon. For the rain brought a misty aura so that the smeary sand seemed to drift forever, the end out of sight and this was just its beginning.

Clifftop

Running can be hard in autumn when the days turn cold so that the air draws in sharp on the lungs and leaves you breathless. At the same time, it is exhilarating, energising and it is with a determined sense of achievement that makes me run up and down the steep path which zigzags its way to the top of the cliff. There is a slight haze hovering over the sand, a sand swept clean by the wash of the waves. Few people walk down below on the beach today. Just a few solitary people walking their dogs.

The paths of life are not always easy, we take the ups with the downs and sometimes we have to struggle to reach the summit and find our way forward. After several climbs I burst out onto the summit where the smooth grass of a park stretches away. Flanked by evergreen oaks it is hard to know that it is autumn. Only the chill gives it away.

Yet I am warm with exertion and a sense of achievement and exhilaration. Running is always therapeutic. Feeling fitness and fresh air flow through every muscle , blood pumping life, the power of pushing the body to its limits, learning new limits and new capabilities. Without challenge we are not pushed and without being pushed we never know our full potential.

Chesil Beach

It is now December and while December

is officially classed as winter from a meterological perspective, traditionally winter does not begin until December 21st, so I have a little leeway, and I love the Chesil, the complete calm and peace which it conjures. I do not know another beach like it.

I crash across the pebbles, each sinking step a thousand scattered sounds shifting with a deeper hollow rip resonating at the force of my footstep which seems to suck me down into an underworld. It is hard work walking on the shingle, ungainly even. I stumble over towards the sea and stop, drinking in the dream, for the atmosphere is always awe inspiring and I become lost in it. Every wave wash whispers permanence, peace, something reassuring.

I could literally sit with a sketch pad or book and listen all day to the breathless sigh of the sea, the water's wash, gently lapping then coming in stronger with a hollow swallowing sound, a watery bony clatter. It continues glugging and lapping until a much larger wave washes in with a roar, fanning out across the Chesil. I am mesmerised by the ever-changing pattern on the pebbles of sea and spume, a kaleidoscope of shapes, the fluidity of form in the body of water which is the sea, sometimes silky smooth, delicately toned with different sea shades, sometimes rolling rough and foamy. I am exhilarated by the undercurrent sucking back with a rasping hiss. These sights and sounds are ancient, this place unique. I wonder how it was formed in the mists of time. Perhaps when the fossils were being laid in the rocks here.

The people of the Bronze Age who erected their small stone circles and buried their dead under tumuli on the ridge above the beach would have also surely looked down upon it in wonder, this long spit of shingle, stretching horizontally across the sea like a manmade island, except that it is natural. I imagine it was there before the giant stones were deposited in nearby stone valley at the end of the ice age, huge boulders strewn across the valley as if hurled by giants. Nothing seems to have been disturbed in this sleepy land and seascape, cows gently graze the green slopes behind the beach as if they have been doing this throughout all time. The 12th century chapel looks on, a beacon from its vantage point, itself ancient yet relatively modern.

I cannot describe sufficiently the joy and the peace that I feel in this place because it overwhelms. There is something so ancient yet timeless, as if time stopped forever, and yet the sea stays in perpetual motion, marking the seconds as it sucks in and out as it has done for millennia. Few shells are cast upon this beach, in fact not a lot is deposited here. Today the shingle is lightly strewn with driftwood; beautiful bark-free branches from trees which grew somewhere else and have been smoothed by the sea as they were carried and caressed on the currents. Light and pale, banded and swirled with shapes from the natural grain, some twisted, some straight, some decorated with worm holes, all smooth and salty to touch, slightly damp and hydroscopic. I place pieces in my pockets, they are beautifully light as if the sea has made them weightless.

Also weightless are the mermaid's purses that are intermittently strewn across the shingle today. Carried quite far in by the tide, most of them desiccated, I imagine they were washed up here a few days hence. I sometimes find them on Bournemouth beach, but very rarely. Today on the Chesil I find ten. Some of them have already been broken by the wind and the shift of the shingle, they lie shrivelled, folded in on themselves skittering away in a breath of breeze which takes them. Feather light they resemble pieces of folded paper, what was once oil-coloured origami, crumpled and creased, tattered and torn. Those intact remain silky smooth, their surfaces brushed with almost imperceptible lines in different tones: black purple, black blue, black brown and black. They resemble giant pieces of ravioli, a neat square pocket enclosing a bulging filling, with the addition of horns which are used to tether the purse to weed under the sea. These are the egg sacks of ray, the species of which I would have to work out from soaking, measuring and looking at the details of each sack, which I do not have the means to do. It is a joy to find them though and never have I seen so many on one day in one place.

Also on the beach are long strands of seaweed in beautiful autumn colours some with roots as if stripped from the seabed and left to lie on the shingle. The seaweeds range from pink, orange and red shades to deep forest purply greens and browns. They tone with large pebbles, sea smoothed and beautifully flat; ovals, circles and some more domed and egg-shaped; heathery purply pink, blue grey and brown. The beautiful natural and neutral colours of the seashore are for me the shades of autumn. Here especially with the shingle which holds an autumnal spectrum in its range of colours from completely black through charcoal greys to browns, purples, orange, red, beige and amber, pale green and cream to snowy white. This array of colour blends together and contrasts the blue grey muted marl of the sea.

Despite this place being timeless and dreamy, dusk is falling. The sea becoming a slumbering shadow, sighing and sinking into itself. From the sound of its sleeper's breath, a gentle exhalation as waves lap the shore, its peaceful presence will still be discerned in the dead of night, even if it blends black with the shadow of the shore. As much as I would like to stay here listening to its nocturnal monologue, I decide to leave, striking out again across the shingle and climbing the slope to the path which will take me to Abbotsbury village. Pheasants sparring in the fields cough and cluck, flapping frenzied wings at each other in head on combat. Their cries continue as I wander past a cowshed, large lantern eyes peering through the dusk light. When they see me, they let out a cow chorus of unmelodious mooing, hoping for food. The pheasants rasp on histrionically. I think of the hunting that happens every autumn on large estates around the area. The snap of shot across silent leaden fields, the rich flavour of game, of autumn.

In the calm of quiet evening, with the anticipation of Christmas, cottages in Abbotsbury glow. The honey stone facades melting into dusk, warm where lights linger on their fading faces. Most houses have a Christmas tree attached to the outer wall on an angled slant, all trees twinkling, casting pools of light onto golden stone. Cottages welcoming, wreaths on doors, curtains still open, reveal their cosy interiors of low-beamed ceilings, log fires and quiet Christmas trees trailed with white lights and lametta. In the big house up the hill, a spacious serenity breathes from within as I see high ceilings and pastel walls adorned with large, gold-framed impressionist paintings of sea and sky. Lamps are lit and the stage is set for an evening of unwinding in front of the fire. The pub looks equally inviting on walking past. A glowing interior set up with wooden tables and chairs, a string of coloured lights winking around the bar, the allure of a pint in front of a roaring fire and a banter with the locals who come with their friendly dogs.

This is the joy of autumn, which shares so many aspects with winter, the hunkering down, the joy of celebration and community, of sharing with strangers, friends and family, of knowing that life goes on and can be enjoyed despite tough and changing times. It is a season of warmth and love, of life as well as death. A season of cosy anticipation, of preparation, of making sure that all those we know, and love will be sustained and provided for when winter comes.

OUT AND ABOUT IN AUTUMN

Hide and seek

I am back in the hide, late autumn. The day seems to sulk beneath bludgeoning clouds, collecting in the higher recesses of the sky like large fists ready to strike. The waters lie languid, trembling with the ethereal, hysterical cry of an oyster catcher and the bubbling cries of a curlew somewhere out in the wash.

The beauty of birdwatching is that you never know what you are going to see, and often I do not know what I am looking at. There is always something new to learn, and watching bird behaviour, these creatures carrying out their daily existence, unperturbed by people, is both relaxing and refreshing, their natural world a therapy and a true escape from an artificial world which never winds down.

Through binoculars I spy a group of ducks; teal and widgeon mainly, congregated in a group. So far out are they, beyond the boundaries of the naked eye, that they appear a small yet significant huddle. Nearer to my naked eye, a red shank steps carefully on long red legs, picking its way

135

through the shallows and eagerly probing the mud with its pointed beak.

Far out again, huddled on an islet of tufted grass, a group of spoonbills have taken up residence. The nature reserve of RSPB Arne where I am stationed, is apparently one of the best places to see spoonbills in the country with a record number of 84 individuals recorded in October 2022. With their tufted heads and cumbersome bills, these birds, which look as if they are wandering around wielding wooden spoons, are unique and comical. Despite the fact that they used to be a prominent feature of British wetlands, their numbers sharply declined due to a combination of land reclamation, hunting and climate change.

I had never seen them before my first encounter with them at Arne, and so it was like love at first sight; I could not take my eyes off them, for they seemed exotic, an attractive curiosity. Now I have got used to them and they are the friendly residents of Arne which always arrive in the autumn to overwinter here. As they are overwintering, and not to my knowledge breeding here, it is unlikely that any teaspoons (as baby spoonbills are affectionately called) will be seen here in the spring. I hope that one day they will establish a colony here as they have in other parts of the country.

Remembrance

It is the lead up to Remembrance Sunday, people wearing their poppies with pride, the familiar face of the simple red paper disc with slightly crimped edges, plastic centre and stalk. If you are lucky, you get one with a green paper leaf. I always sought those ones out as a child and still subconsciously do.

In the recreation ground there is a war memorial listing local names, the young men who died bravely in battle, living out a dystopia to create a relative utopia. On dreary days in November, I would often walk past it, yellow leaves swirling and settling near to the red poppies which decorate the stone plinth. Silence, stillness. Those men are gone now. Names passed on. To their relatives they are the faces, feelings, shared souls, hearts and minds which will never return. Their legacy lives in the shrouded silence of stone, the silence of the cemeteries where they are interred. They must always be remembered.

Remembrance Sunday is a poignant reminder of tragic loss, the loss of lives so young. The cemeteries in northern France and at Gallipoli bring it home. I remember standing horrified, moved beyond measure. Looking out on the beautiful scene of Gallipoli, the azure sparkling sea and the pineclad rolling hills swathed in sunshine and silence. Nature had healed, its zest for life defeating the ugliness of churned up chaos, reckless devastation and death. It had covered the scars, superficially healed the wounds. War seemed distant on that dreamy day which resonated with peace and sunshine and yet the cemetery said it all, speaking volumes in its silence.

The remembrance Sunday schedule works like clockwork in London. The epitome of order in contrast to the chaos of war. The military processions, smart and regimented, no one stepping out of line. I wonder if we could cope with this nowadays in a society which shows less respect for order and discipline, a younger generation which doesn't like to be told. Sombre and dignified. People lost in their own private reflections. The bugle calls at the cenotaph. Speeches are made. Horses parade. There is something comforting about tradition.

Despite its horrors, the war brought about immense change, much of which was positive. With women on the home front, the process of female emancipation was no doubt accelerated as they filled the spaces the men had left behind and proved that they could also be part of the workforce. The war caused an acceleration in communications such as radar, and other technological advances with the concept of the internet even birthed for military communication at this time. Men such as Alan Turing, who is known as the father of computer science, developing algorithms and decoding cipher amongst many other technological advances, helped develop this technology which we take so for granted today. Rebuilding Britain after the war saw the creation of the National Health Service and the Welfare state. And yet the old ways were lost. The decline of country houses and their estates, the loss of land, the dig for victory which turned so much pasture and forest into arable land. As autumn shows in the falling of its leaves, loss is inevitable but so is change.

Urban autumn

A carpet of yellow leaves in the cathedral close lies still until a small child scuffles through them, throwing them into the air with joy as she runs free across the green. I was once that child of three chasing autumn colours. Today is a drab day where grey cold hangs heavy, oppressive as if waiting for something less joyful than the Christmas which Mompesson house awaits. A splendid door- wreath overflowing with evergreen, red ribbons and cinnamon sticks is ready to welcome. Decked and lit, this house, a warm heart on a cold day, is currently closed. Bright bunting buffeted by a cruel wind remains full of hope and promise.

The cathedral stands glorious, glowing. I am drawn into its ever-echoing expanses under lofty vaulted ceilings. Someone is practising the organ, a clash of chords soaring into empty spaces. It is all too big for me, the volume, the familiar scent of stone and polished candles, feathered echoes as solemn as the shadows. Buffeted by many memories, having come here as a child so many times, been such a part of this place, my memories collide like clouds with the organ's spasmodic interludes, chords broken, fragmented phrases, dissonances dominating. They suddenly stop. A breath held in suspense, muffled echoes resonate, slipping away to silence, to nothing. This is modern music. The power and might of everything overwhelming.

Small I stand beneath the ever-reaching columns of fossil-filled Purbeck marble. There is always something new to notice in the ingenious architecture. And this is just manmade, a dedication of worship to God who has accomplished so much more than man could ever do. Tears are the only expression I can muster. I need to get a grip, but the chords come crashing down, their blasts breaking me, shattering something inside me. It is an instrument I have always wanted to master, to feel part of. Gave up too easily, stopped at seventeen, dreams dashed. Now on the outside looking in, staring into the empty spaces, the silences, I have to leave. Composure smiling through tear-stained spaces and fractured light, I walk out. Nobody would ever know how this place affected me.

Respite and recovery in a shop selling gilt frames. Antiquity exuded in the dusty, drawn-out lofty feel of leather-bound libraries where most of these frames probably once hung. This place is a paradise, an enigma. Each frame a new hope and creation, a new idea drawn out for what can fill its empty space. Flowing motifs meld a synthesis of symmetry in different designs. Enveloped in cosy contentment, the pure pleasure of perusal while outside the day is drawn like thick curtains, cold, blank and hostile. Inside is a utopia of fantasy, as if one had stepped back in time to a faded, glorious glamour.

While frames are fripperies, they are inspiring. As golden as the autumn trees and as warming to the heart contrasting the chill outside. They capture my imagination, and my heart finds intense happiness as inspiration strikes its bargain. While I have my imagination, creativity, ideas and inspiration, I will always be intensely happy. For these stimulate the mind to express itself in creative forms. A sense of history and atmosphere are equally compelling, curiosity inducing. The shop has all of this and so is a pure paradise, a place of refuge and recovery on a chill autumn day.

Melting morning

December mist through straight backed trees. Even the lines of commissioned ranks look lovely. Golden pools on needled slopes. A forest of silver birch scintillated in sunlight. Golden tinged tree trunks serried, straight, the flick of sunshine as we hurry past. Open heath where sun burns through fog, and frost lies lightly on grass. Crowns of ancient trees weave into another winter while horses hunker under cold coats, curling breath. Mist is galvanised with gold as if the sky rises forever into a voluminous blurred balloon without focus or dimension.

In the market town, Mozart merges with café clamour, an oasis of elegance in flute and strings, as elegant as those stately trees which still stand time trapped in sunlit fields as they have stood for centuries and past which the bus on which I travelled flashed a half an hour earlier. This is a piece of paradise- watching patterns in the genies which creep from my mug, curling like clouds through the slanting sunshine.

All is bright and optimistic. The robins were singing a duet this morning, each echoing the other on the sun spangled dawn, each seemingly heralding spring which is still so far away. Sunlight spirals through steam or maybe it is the steam spiralling through sunshine. I am caught in time drifting, dreaming, streams of consciousness unleashed as steam wafts with the snippets of Mozart's piano wandering through the soundscape. This drink is too hot to consume quickly; like music and atmosphere it must be savoured. I think of those out in the cold with no hot drink, no such music to elevate the soul, yet the sunshine is sufficient to warm, and the robin's scintillating song surpasses anything manmade. This music is my heritage and yet the birdsong is superior and I long to return to the heath and linger under the trees in the sunshine outside.

Conker contests

While walking along a woodland path, I find a conker face up in the leaf litter. Smooth and shiny, polished like a perfect piece of turned wood with its soft silky grain, it takes me back to childhood. I turn it in my hand like a treasure before slipping it into my pocket, I know that it will wither there if it stays forgotten, that even if I remember to remove it an hour later, that initial glow will have gone. It is almost as if it reflects the childlike enthusiasm and excitement that I feel at the moment of finding it, fast fading after the initial moment has passed.

I remember as children we went to the forbidden field; my brother and I and a couple of school friends. There we searched for conkers amongst leaves and long wet grass beneath the horse chestnut trees. On return, slightly muddy and happy, our pockets bulging with the treasures we had collected; we let our trophies tumble out onto the table with a woody thump. After emptying our pockets, we picked over our prizes; the boys seeking out the biggest, me seeking out the most perfect aesthetically. The boys would fight with theirs, hanging them on strings to slam into each other and so crack the conkers or smash them apart. I found them too polished, too pristine to want to treat them in such a way. They were objects of beauty which I would wrap and put carefully away, always disappointed when unwrapping them to take a tiny peep, that they were already losing their deeply polished sheen. We wondered what ways we could preserve them, but no one knew. The boys would harden them in the Aga after soaking them in vinegar, but this did not preserve their rich lustre, the grain almost wood like which ran serpentine across the surface, and the glow of polished tabletops in an antique shop, or in my grandmother's house which would seem to reflect my smile.

So excited were we by our treasure that we wolfed down cakes and squash, the boys eager to thread the conkers and get back outside for some fun, me eager to wrap my cherished conkers in newspaper and place them somewhere safe. We were so absorbed in our own microcosm, that we were almost resilient to the displeasure of our friends' parents who reprimanded us for going to the field as there could have been strangers there. And so our wonderful world of sweet escape was sullied for a second, pulled back into the real world. It is so sad that society has come to this state, where children are not free to venture too far for fear of others and what they might do. We were fearless then, but it was the adults whose fears fell like autumn leaves into our laps and left us wary.

WOOODLAND WONDERS

Metamorphosis

Early September, the scent of summer still sweet on the heather-honeyed air. Trees are yet to turn, their leaves lingering with the deep chlorophyl of summer, but the rowan has anticipated autumn, already bursting a brilliance of berries; its scarlet jewels being one of the earliest harbingers of the new season. The day drifts in a reverie of calm; docile, warm and gentle as if in a state of nostalgia for summer. Barely a breeze riffles the birch trees, bees still buzz about the heather. But change is on the way, and it is by the small pond on this open heathland where dragon flies dart, that I make a small discovery.

A dragon fly, which I think is a Southern Hawker, is laying her eggs into the bank, her body undulating as she repeatedly pushes her ovipositor into the mud at the water's edge. So engrossed is she in her endeavour that she ignores the dog bounding past, and the fact that I am filming her closely on my phone, capturing this moment. I am in the right place at the right time. This is a once in a lifetime experience and I am privileged to witness such an intimate and important moment in the dragon fly's life as she lays her eggs to create the next generation.

The eggs will stay in the soil, hatching into nymphs (or larvae) in a few weeks or in the spring when they will live in the water, devouring prey such as other insect larvae, small fish and tadpoles. The dragonfly nymph sheds its skin 5-14 times as it grows and its growth, depending on the species, can take up to two years. The final three-hour moult takes place out of the water, and this is when the adult dragonfly emerges. It then lives for about 2 weeks and must mate during that time in order to reproduce itself. This miracle of metamorphosis, so characteristic of many insects, is another of life's small wonders and I find it symbolic for the start of this change to be taking place in autumn which in itself is a time of change.

Tree talk

Autumn is all about trees. The breakdown of sugars in the leaves leading to glorious colours which pierce the gloom on drab days and explode with brilliance on sunny ones. The sursurrance in drying leaves, the squeak of limb as the wind gets up, the wood wide web; that mysterious mycor-rhizal conversation which stirs in the soil and causes symbiosis to thrive.

Two squirrels chase each other around

the trunk of an oak, their claws scratching against thick bark as they scamper up and up, tails bristling, their voices squeaking like rusty hinges. Then one jumps, clean through the air and lands on the branch of an adjacent tree. What agility. These oak trees would know each other, as rooted neighbours, maybe even related. I have heard that trees emit chemical signals to warn neighbouring trees of attack from fungi or pest. In response, the trees which receive the signal give off chemicals to repel or protect against the danger. Different trees have different mechanisms, but they are alive and even without brains can sense and defend themselves, can communicate.

Squirrels are the oak tree's friend, for now the animals are digging in the leaf litter beneath the trees, burying acorns. Jays do an even better job at this and are apparently responsible for the majority of buried acorns. This oak tree, probably about 200 years old, is in its prime of life. It could live for another 600 and during that time will provide a benevolent refuge for a host of flora and fauna whose generations will come and go while the tree lives on. Now in autumn, the eggs of the silver washed fritillary butterfly will be hiding away deep in the crevices of the oak tree's bark, ready to hatch next year. This tree also hosts the purple emperor and purple hair-streak butterflies, spending the duration of their existence up in the leafy canopy so that although these elusive butterflies are native to Britain, hardly anyone has ever seen them. Fungi, fern and moss also make their home on the old tree as do lichen and many an insect. And once the leaves have fallen it is easier to spot the shy tree creepers creeping and crawling their way around the trunk digging out insects from the bark with their long curvy beaks.

There is so much to explore beneath the trees; the hibernating snails, the fungi peering through the leaf litter, discarded leaves, some imprinted with the scaly discs created by gall wasps and others growing the gall itself. These galls were prized in past times for the ink which they produced for writing with. As pigments came from the earth, the ground up minerals from rocks in their autumnal browns, ochres and russet reds, so ink extracted from the autumn gall was also linked to nature. There is something elemental about creating your own paints from natural pigments or your ink from plants. And as an artist I feel passionate about this process, not just for connecting with nature but to feel more at one with the process of creating something from scratch.

Everything seems contained around, beneath and within the embrace of the tree itself, a benevolent being which has stood the test of time and provided an entire ecosystem with sustenance. As the wind stirs in the branches, the flick of dead leaves, twisting and turning as they fall. The tree seems animated, as if, rooted to the spot, it wishes to gesticulate, to elaborate on conversation. The surrounding trees creak and sway in sympathy, inspiring a sense of deep communication in the forest. The squirrels squeaking and scampering in the leaf litter, the whistle of wings as a wood pigeon crashes through the canopy, the cry of rooks and the sighing of the wind through branches, breathing life into the trees themselves, animating them even as they shut down for their winter sleep.

Deer

Sunlight skitters in playful silver shafts down coppiced hazel wands on a dreamy day in October, a breeze riffling the hazels, still clad in large leaves, yellowing. These leaves are for me, one of autumn's delights for they radiate colour, especially on dismal days. As the breeze surges, stirring the leaves to tremble and whisper, sunlight flicks along the length of the coppice wands and daubs dancing dapples on the forest floor. The rich scent of damp leaves and forest earth rises creating a feeling of comfort and warmth.

Coppicing is an ancient practice, barely carried out today, except in nature reserves like this where traditional methods are maintained for sustaining biodiversity. Rather than growing as a tree with a single trunk and a large canopy, a coppiced tree grows up in multiple single shoots which allow more light to penetrate the forest floor than it would through a dense tree canopy, thus enabling spring flowers such as bluebells and wood anemone to flourish. Every five years or so the hazel is cut down on a rotation to roughly 5cm above the coppice stool to encourage several stems (wands) to grow upwards. When tall, the wands are then harvested. In the past they would have been essential provision as an abundant supply of wood for fuel and functional items. Hazel wands were used in basket making and smouldered to make charcoal. Often the wands were woven into hurdles (traditional woodland boundary fences) or used as stakes in hedge laying. I passed some traditional hazel hurdles in a clearing further back, perhaps erected to prevent deer from eating saplings there.

Deer are ubiquitous in the British Isles. Without any predators such as wolves or lynx, they pose a threat to biodiversity through the simple fact that they have voracious appetites. The consumption of woodland scrub, which makes essential nesting places and food sources for many species of bird, as well as providing nectar for butterflies, has been partly responsible for the reduction in bird numbers in species such as the nightingale and turtle dove. In addition, the consumption of saplings prevents forest regeneration, especially in areas where forests are being replanted. It is with sadness that I often encounter saplings growing up inside long plastic protective tubes, leaves peering over the top as if desperately finding freedom. While the trees themselves are protected, the plastic shield that protects them poses an alternative threat to the environment.

The alternative to these plastic protected trees is perhaps deer stalking, a popular British pastime. This is sadly argued necessary to manage deer numbers and protect habitat loss. The autumn countryside rings with the shot of hunters and men in wax jackets, green wellies and Harris tweed caps (deerstalkers) can be seen parking their four by fours up at the roadside in remote places brandishing rifles and flasks of tea ready for a morning's hunt. Most of this shooting is probably after pheasants. The iridescent feathers of the male being predominantly orange and russet, as well as the beautifully banded tail feathers in shades of brown are for me the epitome of autumn.

Coming out of the copse into a bright woodland clearing is an assault to the eyes. Sunshine blazes on soft springy pasture flanked by forest and hedgerow. For the first few moments I blunder across it, somewhat dazed until my eyes grow accustomed to the brilliance of natural light. Breeze riffles in hawthorn hedges studded with bright berries, sleepy sloes or otherwise blackthorn berries hang adjacent, their large inviting clusters powdered with bloom. This abundance of berries sustains the birds. Although I do not see any actually eating them today, I can discern some of their calls on the air; a robin sings from a bush, the brilliance of its spangled sound as bright as the sunlight. A chiff chaff still sings on this October day. Very soon it will be leaving for sunnier, warmer climes migrating all the way to Africa. The miracle of migration with autumn being the catalyst. While it is sad to see the departure of swifts and swallows, whose flitting flights and needle thin calls laced the skies of summer and are now but a beautiful memory, new arrivals will steal the show and I could personally spend all day lost in a hide by the mudflats on the coast, watching the waders come and go. Yet here deep in the Hampshire countryside, field birds take centre stage; redwings and fieldfares, both of the thrush family, taking up residence so that there is almost something soothing about seeing flocks of them in the fields, the red marks on the redwing especially suited to the autumn and winter seasons. Waxwings are another bird which migrates to the UK countryside, and although I look out for them, I have never seen one.

I walk through the meadow, cross the road and into ancient downland where a completely different habitat thrives. The sunshine illuminates seedheads from the faded flowers of summer, with the wild carrot being the most striking. I love its umbelliferous form, the strength of its structure. This part of downland seems to sing, alive with the chattering of gold-finches as they indulge in these precious seeds. The lack of seedheads on modern farms are another cause for the decline in field birds, but out here in the wild downland which has been here undisturbed since the brink of time, the birds find their feast.

Undulating downs golden in the sunlight are ablaze with berries on small scrub bushes which dot the landscape. More food for birds. Sheep graze, their bleating carrying far across the landscape where they appear as little dots, white flecks on a golden backdrop of downland grass. All over this ancient landscape weave the long lines of iron age earthworks intersecting, wandering far out to the horizon. Their banks are clad with dense foliage which have turned the most beautiful collision of colours- crimson, purple, yellow orange and brown woven with wispy old man's beard and looped with languid chains of the black bryony, adorning the bushes like beads. The black shapes of sloes and the red of hawthorn all combine in a rich medley of autumn in both colour and texture.

I wander in the dreamy downs on this exquisite early autumn day, still warm enough for the odd butterfly to be about, the final flowers of scabious to still be flourishing, and then retrace my steps to the meadow across the road and back towards the copse. This time on the air comes the wild mewing of a buzzard coursing the currents. I see its shape floating on the thermals of an eternal blue. Then the unmistakeable hoarse grunt of a rutting stag emanates somewhere deep in the forest. His call comes in waves, almost inaudible and then comes closer, more pronounced so that while I was initially not sure if I were dreaming, I am later sure he is there, hidden by the trees.

There are definitely deer in these forests. I have seen them myself on many occasions, usually in the form of a shy doe slipping silently through the trees. Elusive as a phantom flicking past, a figment of the imagination, so stealthily does she go, unseen but all seeing. A beautiful creature, shy, secretive, enigmatic, gentle and clever. It seems so sad to think that these lovely animals might have to be culled, although I hear no gunshots here. Perhaps the hazel hurdles serve their purpose in saving the scrub and saplings by keeping the deer at bay. In summer there are apparently nightingales and turtledoves singing here.

Fungi

One of the major allures of autumn are the fungi. Their mysterious micro-cosms beneath the earth, helping trees to exchange clandestine conversations, collect nutrients, to break down and be recycled once dead. Hyphae run ghost-like through the forest floor, within dead wood, and appear suddenly, spectrally on the surface, manifesting as fruiting bodies, their only strange and short-lived appearance in the external world.

I find fungi fascinating; their multifarious shapes and forms, from great goblets and parasols to tiny delicate porcelain lamp-shades, dinner plates, domes and spiky coral-like fingers reaching for the sky. The collection of colours is equally impressive, ranging from brown through the spectrum of purples, russets, reds, yellows and orange. Some fungi are even purply pink. But it is the blue elf cup fungi which really eludes me. The tantalising turquoise tint found on the dead wood of oak trees revealing its secret presence, the fact that it once fruited, staining the wood. This stained wood has, in turn been used through the centuries to decorate and inlay furniture.

It took ten years before I finally found them one day on a woodland walk, suddenly staring straight up at me, elusive elf cups, turquoise and tangible. Brilliant to behold, these tiny cups are a complete wonder. I have never seen anything of this intensity and of this particular colour in the natural world, apart from the kingfisher's fleeting back, the streak of turquoise which follows the needle thin call as the kingfisher suddenly appears from its secret perch amidst the autumn leaves.

As I felt when I found the fossil sea urchin, stumbling upon the unexpected for which I had been searching so long is a sensation of ecstasy which I cannot describe. My eyes couldn't take in enough of these elf cups, I couldn't believe what I was seeing, and yet there they were, living out their secret, secluded lives underneath a piece of wet and dead wood. The only hint of their presence had been a slight bluish tint, a stain in the water-soaked wood. Turning over revealed the treasure, a secret cash of tiny turquoise cups. I felt an immense feeling of satisfaction that I had finally found what I was looking for all these years, that the forest had not entirely eluded me, and that these fairytale forms did actually exist, despite being not that common.

Fungi fuse with folklore. As a child I was fascinated by the fairy rings which suddenly sprang up on our lawn. I dug beneath them, hoping to chance upon a subterranean world of fairies and phantasy. I was warned to never touch or try as fungi have the power to poison and even kill, so I held a healthy respect but was always eager to enter into their world, that weird and wonderful world which we know nothing about but stood as an intense source of fascination. Today I feel exactly the same. No longer looking for fairies, but eager to learn more about these elusive lives which put in such a short appearance above ground yet live long underground, harbouring their secrets under the soil.

The fruiting bodies are fungi in their full glory. They are aliens entering our realm. Saprophytic, strange, hallucinogenic, bioluminescent, attracting, alluring, enticing an evocative sense of wonder. Indeed they are one of the world's wonders, so integral yet so alien, so important yet so destructive. They have established a symbiosis with much of the natural world, yet they can control vast areas and lay it to waste, such as the aggressive honey fungus which preys like a pathogen across vast areas, consuming its hosts.

And so I stand in awe, while the wind steals through the trees, leaves flicking down to bed in the leaf litter through which peeps many fungal forms if you look closely and carefully. Hours engrossed in their tiny world puts our own into perspective, provides a sense of escape into a world which is so far beyond the realms of our imagination yet exists here on earth.

Slime moulds

Slime moulds, once considered close relations to the fungi world, are perhaps even more weird and wonderful, often appearing as bright jewels on dying wood or as slicks of what only can be described as vomit. They are not infact fungi at all, but plasmodial structures created from single celled organisms called protists. So strange are they that there is still much to learn about them that I wonder why we spend so much time and money looking for life in space when there is still so much to learn about the strange and alien life forms on our own planet.

I have heard that slime moulds can walk, not with legs obviously, but using the process of chemotaxis where they sense chemicals in their environment and move either away or towards them. This allows them to seek out food sources. It is hard to describe the excitement of finding something for the first time, something which has existed secretly for my entire life and yet I never noticed it was there. This was what happened when I first encountered orange sporangia slime mould. It was actually in winter, looking like a pile of eggs which could have been laid by an insect waiting secluded in the closet of a knot of wood before they hatched in spring. But they were not eggs but slime moulds, huddled together, bright like beads of plastic. As with the elf cups, it is noticing the little things that really excite, the discovering something new; a simple pleasure which brings so much joy.

Lichen

I can't say much about lichen other than I am intrigued by it, just in the same way that I am intrigued by moss, slime moulds and fungi. After a storm, lichen, which has been growing densely on the branches of trees and hidden from sight, often falls to the ground. We find it in multifarious shapes and forms strewn across the forest floor and when looked at close up, it takes on structures, shapes and textures like a wondrous piece of embroidery. Some forms are leafy, crinkly, almost cruciferous, others are like long tentacles or hair, some are structured into cellular shapes which fit together in interlocking patterns and others are like little trumpets rising out of the lichen's "leafy" backdrop. These are the forms which I have looked at closely with my macro. There are many more.

Lichen are a fusion of fungi with either algae or cyanobacteria, the latter two being known as photobionts, having the ability to photosynthesise, which allows the fungal part of the lichen to obtain food. It is thought that this is a symbiotic relationship, and that the photobiont also benefits in some way from the environment which the fungi provides, but not all scientists agree that there are mutual benefits and that the fungi fare better. This apparent symbiosis has nevertheless created what appears to be a new form of life, a metamorphosis of fungi as it fuses with another organism and so creates a hybrid, so intricate and complex in shape and form and so essential to the ecosystem in its own right. I find this mind-blowing.

I love looking at lichen in autumn when it seems to proliferate on the branches of shrubs and trees. Much of it is grey green but some species are white, amber or even yellow. Growing on the branches of hawthorn, when sunstruck, the blush of red berries strike a brilliant chord beside these bright yellow lichen, enhancing the feeling of autumn and the richness of colour which it provides.

Vernditch forest

The blaze of beech leaves and the sunken silence as I wander through woodland on a cold November afternoon is compelling. The sky a soft pastel blue alluding to an indiscernible sun is a soft as the leaf litter underfoot, the crunch and mulch of beechnuts amid a myriad leaves. More drift down silently like snow. The all-embracing silence and solitude is comforting, contained, I am alone with life in the forest, the birds which are heard but not seen, the animals which sleep in burrows deep beneath the earth, the hibernators, those that walk by night, none of them seem threatening. In the silent spread of calm, spreading like the canopy of beech above, I know that everything will be alright.

Time is said to be healing, although every second seems like a step further away from farewells, it can also be seen as a step nearer a reunion. Life is like that. The glass is either half full or half empty, it is what you make of it. The cycle of the seasons are inevitable as is loss, but however painful, it can also be positive as we learn resilience. I look at my reflection in puddles on the path, see something of myself caught in the bright background of dying leaves; I feel like a phoenix rising from the flames.

The trees are in their prime, their autumn glory. Even as time passes, they seem to say that with age, life only gets better. Trees bear fruit in autumn and bask in a beautiful golden serenity as if sustained by experience and wisdom. In a world obsessed with youth and vanity, a world which constantly strives to live longer, bombarding us with solutions to defy age and death. In a world which holds little respect for the elderly, the autumn leaves seem to hold a secret respect in their simple display of playful brilliance.

The forest steps out onto an ancient drove, a path cutting through the countryside down which people passed as if on pilgrimage to visit the cathedral in the vibrant city where they could also sell their livestock. This path was part of their journey, just as it is part of mine at this moment. If only trees could talk, telling the tales about the people who passed by here once and have passed on. A blackbird bustles in the hedgerow, sending out a chuttering of annoyance, a robin sings, its shrill song is one of fresh clarity and hope. These things will always be, here and constant, despite the changes of the seasons, the changes in life. The cliché goes, life is a journey, and we all walk along its path. My steps renew their vigour.

I cut back into the wood, wandering with a happier heart. There is so much to be thankful for and the woodland looks beautiful, magnificent in its defiance of decay and its blaze of glory. For death is defeated here, the leaves are merely being shed as we shed skin, the trees remain stoic, surviving through the seasons and the centuries as they have always done, and life will return in spring.

The trees are completing their cycle, just as the cycle of the seasons, the cycle of life to new life and the day to night. And so as the moon rises in the pallid sky and the soft shadows of dusk drift down, I exit the woodland and wend my way back home.

Paper's provenance

The papery swirl of maple leaves, beautiful colours colliding, curling, floating, falling all around. It reminds me of the mail, a jumbled assortment of post falling through the letter box every morning. We would wait eagerly as my mother sifted through the boring brown business envelopes with windows and the white ones, to see if there were any exciting letters from friends.

Most days I would receive one, an envelope which stood out as a distinct colour. For we wrote on different coloured papers, sometimes pastel, sometimes bright, reflecting the mood or personality of the sender. In those days when we sent letters, we would put so much thought and care into choosing papers to reflect our identities. We would mix and match colours to clash or coordinate accordingly: a plain pastel green with a pale blue like spring skies, an orange explosion with bright pink, or maybe a mellow yellow or red like the trees of autumn.

As a teenager I preferred to write on dark colours; wine red or indigo or black with silver stars embossed in the corners. I always wrote with silver or gold ink. Letters from penfriends in France, written in neat blue biro or sometimes cartridge pen, were always on white paper printed with small motifs. The letters from my penfriends in Germany were always grey, newspaper thin, recycled unbleached with a discrete design printed in a subdued colour to make the paper more original. This paper intrigued me because they all wrote on the unbleached grey. They also always wrote in school cartridge pen blue ink with cursive script which seemed to flow like the leaves drifting down in their curling paths. Germans were into recycling long before the British. Being very environmentally aware as a teenager, I marvelled at their innovation, how old paper could be transformed into new, an amazing metamorphosis. But even before that stage of recycling, paper was a product of transformation, once being wood from trees which are so prominent in autumn.

The first use of wood, pulped to make paper, occurred in 1840 in Germany. Before that, the pulp would have come from rags made of linen and hemp. These rags would have been soaked and then beaten and pulped, pressed and then dried. Paper was also sometimes made from tree bark or plant fibres such as papyrus, a true metamorphosis of substance translating from its natural form into something manmade, like sand into glass.

We have lost something today by not sending letters, an art of thoughtful communication purposed by pen, for people took time to write, to think about what they were going to say, their messages were personal, special, not just something pinged off at the drop of a hat in response to something electronic. Although modern communication is effortless and revolutionary, it lacks something of the personal touch and the sense of excitement which came with receiving something thoughtful through the post.

As the leaves fall down, I think of how time has fallen away, changed as the seasons change and the trees lose their leaves. We cannot bring back the past, the times when we wrote letters, spent all our pocket money at stationery shops on coloured papers and perfumed inks, decorated pencils and coloured pens. We got excited about stamps which were steamed off and kept in an album; celebration stamps to mark historical moments which came out much more regularly than today. Yet surely the joy of collecting, keeping and communicating are all essential aspects of autumn which as important as they were then, continue in a transformed way in modern times.

Hatfield forest

Sunlight sifts through the turning, trembling leaves of an ancient oak tree. The morning is cold, crisp, misty. Breath lingers in plumes on chilled air, and I watch the shadowy forms of a group of fallow deer gently grazing in a clearing. Hatfield is a medieval royal hunting forest, established in 1100 and apparently one of the most intact in the country. Hunting forests were established in the Middle Ages and reserved exclusively for royal hunting. Nearer to home lies the New Forest, also an ancient hunting forest from the time of William the Conqueror, and Cranborne Chase (of which Vernditch forest mentioned above is a part) and which was used by King John.

Hatfield forest was my paternal grandfather's favourite place to walk. Situated at Bishop's Stortford, Essex, a short drive from his home, he would step out with walking stick at a slow regular plod. At the age of eighty, he was still clocking 3 miles a day. I had many a good walk with him and my grandmother (and often with my family as well) wandering in the wood pastures and studying some of the ancient trees which have grown in Hatfield for centuries.

Under the National Trust the forest is managed in the old ways of coppicing and pollarding. Ancient trees are also cared for. Forest law stated that only royalty could hunt here, however, when those laws were disbanded, the forest could be used by commoners. This also happened in the

New Forest, which as far as I know is the only place in the UK where commoners are still allowed to graze their animals, cows, pigs, ponies and donkeys.

The beech trees, always the most stunning trees in autumn, are flaming bronze, copper and yellow. I love to crunch through the beech mast which collects in deep swathes of fallen leaves. Beech nuts were consumed by commoners and seen as a nutritious food source. They were also fed to pigs and other domestic animals as pannage, along with acorns which the pigs would root out as they foraged the forest floor, aerating the soil and helping the ecosystem.

Hatfield is a special place, with peace pervading its pastures and forest clearings, a sense of history always present. Somewhere in the forest is a bench dedicated to my grandfather, an act of love and remembrance gifted by my grandmother after he died. His memory lives on in this precious place which was his favourite.

The New Forest

I have come to a village in the New Forest where my ancestors lived for at least 400 years. Ponies, as everywhere in this forest, wander the smooth grass verges along the side of the road. The New Forest, like every medieval hunting forest, consists of wood pastures and pockets of trees. One such pocket grows near the village where I am heading. I see an old oak, maybe 400 years old, its back twisted and limbs contorted. I wonder if my ancestors looked upon the same tree.

The New Forest normally feels gentle and peaceful, an internationally important place for wildlife, including some which is very rare. Streams meander through its interior and I am lulled by the trickling sound of moving water, trees turn beautiful copper colours and pigs and ponies mainly wander the paths and pastures. There are often donkeys too, moody looking (a little like the ponies) but tolerate a gentle stroke or pat. There are several smart towns, in one of which a friend of mine took a wonderful photo of a cow crossing the road on the zebra crossing with such nonchalance that the traffic had to halt. The New Forest is full of small villages and pubs with thatched roofs and is generally a popular place for weekends and families, nature and recreation. But there is something quaint about it, a feeling of unease and I certainly felt it today.

The village I had come to see, where my ancestor in the 17th century owned land which he portioned out to family members in his will along with money, seemed not to exist. A ribbon development of large Victorian houses with imposing iron gateways shutting people out was all that I could see. The church was nowhere to be seen and there was no pub and no heart. Property in the New Forest tends to be exclusive and expensive and many people who live there have moved in from outside, although there are also many families who have been commoners on the land for generations, managing the land and understanding the eco system.

It was when I had exhausted walking the village from end to end and we drove someway out that I spotted the old church, out on a limb. It was locked. We passed a swanky golf club beautifully manicured and maintained and went and had a pint at a small pub where two donkeys, who didn't mind being stroked, were hanging about outside. The New Forest is a strange fusion of humble tradition and opulence, of locals and those from outside, of those who come here for wildlife and walking and those who visit to seek entertainment and spend money. It is a fusion which, to my mind, can never truly marry or settle comfortably and therefore leaves a sense of disequilibrium and change.

Storm

There is something so exciting about a storm, all-consuming compelling. I watch from my window as the wind races and roars through the oak trees, tearing limb from limb, sending leaves to tumble and fall. An energy unleashed with exhilaration which enlivens the senses has me mesmerised so that I could sit and watch the wind whipping the trees all evening, the stars flicking between their moving branches as the clouds course across.

It is cosy and contained in my warm room but all too often I will go out walking in it to feel its full impact, to become connected, immersed, the rasp of rain on my face, the wind in my hair. I always prefer to be on the inside, at the heart of something rather than standing outside, being left out, a spectator on the outside looking in. That is why I have never been interested in following anyone on social media, watching other people's lives. For the same reason, I dislike superficial relationships or being a tourist. The storm excites and exhilarates, I return soaked to the skin and abundantly happy. I have been hit on the head with acorns and pelted with wet leaves. This is the autumn equinox and out in the dark, the light of streetlamps rises and falls with the moving shadows of the wind in the trees.

I am left laughing because I can always come back to the warm winking lights of home and security. Yet the storms of life can be cruel, unnerving, The ups and downs of life's rollercoaster with its hopes and fears. Fear of change; of loss, of losing love, friends falling away; of dreams left to drift and die; of death itself, or the reality of any of these things. As the storm causes leaves to fall, they too are forever lost, each unique, irreplaceable. When we fall, we are also lost, helpless even.

In the morning I go out, standing amongst the litter, the wreckage of broken branches, empty acorn cups, tattered twigs and leaves left to lie in dying drifts. Raindrops tremble like tears on twigs which have been left exposed, stripped bare, their leaves lying like piles of clothes on the forest floor. In the stillness of the aftermath there is time to think, to reflect, to pray. In a world which pursues happiness above all else, there is apparently no room for sadness, yet surely it is essential for the soul, for self-development, resilience, perseverance and strength. We can never be endlessly happy, that is the world's cruel lie.

A robin's bright and optimistic notes reflect this strength in its perseverant melody. It speaks of resilience, hope, new life, rebirth and reminds us that spring will soon come. The trees will take on new leaves and be clothed in a bright, fresh optimism. The world will be looked at differently in a new light, from a different perspective, things will have moved on. Every loss saddens the heart, every fear causes it to miss a beat, and yet we learn to prepare, adapt and survive. This is surely the lesson which autumn teaches as we watch the squirrels store their acorns away, the women pickling preserves in traditional villages and the harvest being gathered in.

NIGHT LIFE

Harvest Moon

Driving back from a rehearsal, travelling through the countryside, my father and I notice the full moon rising in the sky. We have been playing Bach cantatas all day, he on cello and I on viola. It has been a day of dreams; beautiful words combined with emotive melodies and harmonies, the wonderful connection which flows between all musicians as we each play our parts. In the space of that school hall and in that moment of time we become a unit, the heartbeat and synchronised breath of an organism whose common passion is to play the music and convey its emotion and meaning to the best of our ability, to give the audience joy. I have been playing music for many years, and it never ceases to delight, inspire, exhilarate. It never loses its power to draw me in and keep me captivated, to lose myself in my imagination, to be elevated to new heights. The shared experience with fellow musicians always guarantees to give me a buzz so that I find it very hard to come back down to earth.

The moon is rising, and we are both buzzing, my father and I, reliving the moment with the wandering ear worms of Bach's blissful melodies. Yet the moon transports us further, for it is otherworldly, another wonder outside ourselves. As the sun is just setting, the moon hangs on the horizon above the fields, a bloated amber orb, an optical illusion, surreal, distorted, bent by the atmosphere, appearing much larger than it actually is. The atmosphere plays tricks, its density bending the light and changing the colour. During the journey home the massive moon will rise and shrink yet still remain larger than usual, giving off a more focussed piercing light. The Harvest Moon.

The Harvest Moon is the nearest full moon to the autumn equinox, rising either in September or early October. It rises as the sun sets and therefore is always present in the night sky. So called because traditionally it was by its light that the farmers could work later into the night to collect the harvest.

As we drive along the avenue of 365 Beech trees on the Blandford to Wimborne road planted in 1835 By the William John Bankes of Kingston Lacy to honour his mother, the Harvest Moon is rising between their branches. Colourful beech leaves subdued by the shadows of night, only illuminated by the car's headlights which also reveal deep shapes and shadows on the tree trunks, knots in the wood become faces, the trees take on personalities, telling tales, their "faces" seem to move with the shift of shadow and light as our passing headlights pan across the silky surface of the bark, their gesticulating branches seem to wave.

I remember the moon rising above the ancient hillfort of Badbury Rings over to our left. The large pink face peeping over the ridge of a rampart, silently rising, mysterious, awesome. It filled me with fascination and inspiration. I thought beyond the confines of this ancient earth and into a whole new realm. It was something too big for me. That was not the Harvest Moon but occurred late one summer when the air was still sweet with grasses which waved and glowed in the backlight of the setting sun.

By the time we get home, a drive of about 40 minutes from north Dorset, the Harvest Moon has risen beyond its bleary-eyed awakening. It is now looking down, fully focussed and bright, its still silent silver light flooding the fields and the ancient places, filling my small garden with a pool of light, magical, mesmerising. Yet haughty and hostile, it watches from afar, riding behind the clouds and out into the clear and empty spaces of the sky. It does not have the warm benevolence as it had when it hugged the horizon earlier in the evening, yet I am drawn to it, and after my father has left to go home, I go outside and stand in its silver scintillation, letting the light flow over my fingers while Bach earworms in my head.

In 2024 the Harvest Moon was a supermoon, as was the Hunter Moon later in October and the Beaver Moon in November. Three supermoons in autumn that year.

The Hunter Moon

The Hunter Moon is the first full moon to occur after the Harvest Moon. If the Harvest Moon occurs in September, then the Hunter follows in October. If the Harvest is in October, the Hunter follows in November. I have heard that huntsmen used to take advantage of the light of this full moon to hunt at night, to gather game for winter which they could hang from the rafters or dry and salt. This gathering, preparation, this survival against death is just as the farmers did at harvest. Our ancient ancestors who relied on rural and agricultural communities to sustain them would have placed much more significance around autumn than we do today. As we buy most of our provisions from the super-market, it is perhaps too easy to forget the hard work which putting food on the table actually requires. I have a long-lasting respect for our farmers and the constant challenges that they face from global competition, finances, weather, govern-ment. Maybe we should be more mindful of buying local produce, local vegetables in season and local meat. After all, there can be nothing more comforting that a hearty casserole in autumn, full of root vegetables when the trees start to turn, the first frost covers everything in crystals and the cold comes in to bite.

Beaver Moon

The Beaver Moon, called because in the strength of its light, beavers in Canada and America are apparently more active busily building their dams and storing food for winter. I imagine them under the moon-light, slipping nonchalantly into the water, the silver light swilling around them in outgoing ripples, silver skimming their wet backs. As they swim, they leave a trail of streamlined silver water in their wake. I have seen this on documentaries many times as they carry branches between their teeth having gnawed through a few trees. They are very strong and industrious, savvy survivors and work hard to provide for their families who will winter it out under the water in the cosy recesses of their dams.

Autumn in Canada is renowned for its beauty, the national tree, the maple, resplendent in its vibrant intensity of colour. Winters are harsh and cold, and beavers need to work hard to prepare. Despite being nocturnal, many documentaries have also shown them swimming by day on placid lakes, colliding with the colours of the autumn trees which reflect in a marbled swirl of orange, yellow and red. It all seems idyllic as the beavers cruise through the currents, blissfully at home in the water, making everything seem so easy. They are the second largest rodents after the capybara and have the similar small eyes (accustomed to night vision) and waterproof coat.

I wonder if the moon has the same effect on the British beavers which are now thriving in many small populations in secret locations, little enclaves of animals perhaps beavering through the night in the moonlight. Somehow, I feel that the moon shines less here, that it is perhaps not as large or strong, that it is more frequently covered by cloud, but I might be wrong. British winters tend to be mild, thanks to the Gulf stream, and perhaps beavers here do not have to prepare themselves as much. I know that such animals exist in enclaves not far from where I live and there are reports that some have broken free and colonised in the wild. However, I have never seen them. I would love to. A much-maligned animal, beavers are definitely making a comeback as they are nature's engineers and have been proven positive for the environment, regulating water courses, stopping floods, helping aquatic wildlife to thrive. In a time when the climate is changing and we are suscep-tible to more rainfall, they will perhaps become more important for keeping our ecosystems alive.

Trick or treat

Part of the fun of fancy dress is to be outside before bedtime, looking as scary as possible and bribing adults for lots of sweets. That is the fun of Halloween for many young children. A walk around the nocturnal neighbourhood at a time when one is usually thinking about bed sets the tone for the excitement of the evening. But it is the darkness that really thrills, when everything familiar to daytime seems transformed, taking on new sizes and shapes. Houses loom large, their windows warm and glowing, their front doors standing tall as one walks out of the shadows and reaches for the bell. Under the streetlights silent shadows sway beneath silhouette trees, waiting. Sometimes a fox will steal a hungry look, slinking down the street and away into the night, retreating into the comfortable shadows of the wheelie bins which wait in serried rows on corners. Cat's eyes gleam cold and large from unexpected places. It is probably the neighbour's cat but in the darkness, it looks larger, less furry and friendly. The children huddle together in a mass of excited laughter and walk on together.

The children probably don't realise that Halloween is a celebration of death. Falling on 31st October, it coincides with many other festivals of death around the world. In Mexico the day of the dead (1st November) is a time to reconnect with ancestors and visit their graves with offerings of food and drink. The Celtic festival of Samhain (October 31st and November 1st) was a recognition of going from summer into the darker part of the year, a connection with the dead through feasting and drinking (ancient burial tombs would sometimes have been opened up). But less known, is that a study of the ancient Hebrew calendar which begins its year in September, shows that the day of Noah's flood when most of mankind was swept away by the rising waters also occurred on this day. The second month in the Jewish calendar coincides apparently with October 14th and the flood occurred on the 17th day of the 2nd month, according to Jewish scripture, which results in the flood commencing on the 31st October.

For the little children who wander the streets with sweets, it is a time of innocent fun, and I have not heard of many tricks being played around here. As children we were not encouraged to take part, for why should we demand something for nothing and then punish people (usually adults) for not getting what we wanted. My mother would always answer the door armed with a clove of raw garlic which she would give instead of sweets saying it would keep the evil spirits at bay!! Strangely, not many trick or treaters visited our house. Perhaps it was the long, potholed drive, which presented a risk for twisting ankles in the dark, or our large black labrador who hated anyone coming to the door and once leapt through the window at the postman, that put them off. Still, it is a good excuse to dress up.

Fireworks

The days are drawing in ever earlier. I stand under a clear sky where a waxing gibbous moon ebbs into the voluminous dome of evening; a phantom filigree form of pale beaten gold streaked with shadows as clouds wave their wispy banners in front of its face. Shards of sunlight fall into fragments of fading daylight, reflecting in Georgian townhouse windows, soon to be extinguished completely like candles snuffed. Yet it is not time to climb the creaky spiral stairs to bed. Five o'clock and night has descended yet the day is not done.

Blackbirds chip the dusk with their comfortable calls, a dusk which draws itself like a velvet cape around us all. For them it is time to roost, as with all diurnal creatures, to become comfortable and cosy amongst the dying leaves and bare branches. The streets seem to echo with their calls, and the footsteps of people purposefully walking. Yet the evening is stretched with a stillness, as if it calmly waits for something, suspended in silence.

A firework bangs, a shower of stars crackling through the sky from somebody's back garden. A tense excitement grips the air, a wonder which still captivates, childlike. A dog barks. Excitement in the stillness, more tension. I remember the firework displays of childhood; a friendly field with local families who had all put a few pounds into the pot for the village display. It was always bitterly cold, hands and feet throbbing so that after the display we wanted to get indoors as quickly as possible. There was none of the sophistication of coordinated synchronised displays, loud lights, music and a fun fair to keep us there all evening as there is today. As usual, things have become expensive, impersonal and too commercial.

In our garden we would build a big bonfire. My dad had been building it for months; all the dregs and dross from pruning and mowing, the detritus of gardening over the last year. It would tower several meters high, a huge unwieldy stack. Health and safety was far from everyone's minds then, although as children we were always supervised when it came to lighting fireworks. There was something of the pyromaniac in us as we stood at arm's length with a fiery taper excited to set off a big bang, delighted by the boom as a rocket propelled itself into the night air laced with a crack, a bang and a delirious dazzle of stars scintillating delicious trails of gunpowder. As the sound died away, the night would become silent again, secret and mysterious, illuminated only when we sent more stars shooting up into its empty interior.

Breathlessly, we swirled sparklers, wonder crackling and dancing against the black beyond. It was all-absorbing, euphoric. There is always something so exciting about being outside at night, by illuminations. Illuminating the night brings about a cosy security, the promise of warmth, of safety, although a fire is anything but safe. Perhaps it was the combination of reckless freedom in the playing with fire, and the fact that we were in control, and felt completely safe in the company of our parents and other adults. Perhaps it was even something in the subconscious from the times of our ancestors who gathered around fires to eat and share stories.

In preparation for Bonfire Night, my brother and I always made a guy, a stuffed pair of tights with a floppy head, looking more like a scarecrow. He would sit astride the bonfire, being consumed while we consumed sausages and jacket potatoes, and our mum plied us with home-made soup. Our neighbours would join us every year, climbing through the yew arch in the hedge which separated our properties. They had two teenage daughters who I looked up to immensely, always wishing I could be like them. Our big black Labrador would not want to miss out. Food outdid any fear of fireworks and if he thought there was a sausage to be had, he would be there despite the frenzy of fire and flame lighting up the night sky against the backdrop of trees, the cracks and bangs and showers of stars.

Fireworks are not a new custom. Rockets and Catherine wheels in the time of Elizabeth the 1st were on a gigantic scale. I recently watched a documentary by Lucy Worseley recreating a firework display which was performed for Elizabeth the 1st. As well as the huge Catherine wheels, which were cartwheels covered in small rockets sending scintillating sparks to trail out into the furthest recesses of the night, there were huge rockets which propelled comet-like clouds up into the air, and fizz-gigs which whirred around in demented frenzies, completely out of control and not knowing which direction they would take. There was also a huge dragon which descended a line, rockets in its mouth and coming from under its tail, it propelled its way as if on a zip wire. Such extravagance is the mark of another time. There was something larger than life yet unsophisticated, and the wonder which went with it must have been the same. For most people would have never seen such spectacles and it must have been amazing to behold, as one feels when one sees the stars or a comet in the night sky.

Our psychedelic displays, timed and coordinated with special effects are truly taking firework displays to a new level, but we perhaps marvel more at the precision and the creativity of colours and textures which have been placed together, rather than the fact that we can shoot stars into the sky. We expect sophistication today, not wonder. Technology has created this, there is nothing new to discover and everything can be explained. Therefore, I think we have also lost so much appreciation for the simple things, which in autumn are in abundance.

Walking

It is now November, and the weather has taken a twist towards winter. Cold and clear, the night sparkling with as many stars that can be observed in a built-up area. Venus hangs halfway above horizon's line, big and bright, a glittering, multi-faceted diamond. Delicate fronds of silver birch breathe as the breeze stirs them, delicate, ethereal in the dusk-light. Blackbirds chip and chisel at the fading light with their comforting chinking calls, they are preparing to roost. Soon birdsong will fall silent, only the robin remains sitting under a streetlight singing its jingle-jangle song. It will continue like this well into the night.

As the diurnal birds retreat to the trees to spend the night within their bare branches, nocturnal creatures take to the night. An urban fox skulks in the shadows away from the streetlights, looking warily over its shoulder as we pass. It slinks up a sideroad and disappears into someone's front garden.

Christmas is coming early this year with many houses already draped with dazzling lights. There are lights twisted around tree trunks in people's gardens and framing the front of houses. But it is the deep dark wood beyond the houses which holds my fascination, for from it come the cries of a female tawny owl, the wild kerwick, kerwick as she sets off on a night adventure. The shadows of the forest are her secret spaces, her trees tinged monochrome, her colourless autumn experience sensed; the cold crispness fluffing her feathers, the minutest rustles of dry leaves beneath her, easily revealing the presence of her prey as they move across them. Her haunting cries are ethereal, reassuring that there is a natural world out there beyond the decorated trees.

The oak trees near my house have shed their leaves. They lie in dry piles, pushed by the breeze so that they scuffle and shuffle along the path with a comforting soft scratching sound. And then I hear a regular rustle, so light and soft that I realise a cat is also out, delicately padding across the piles of dry oak leaves, their presence presented in the soundscape, just like the rodents which they and the owl are looking to catch. Like snow, dry leaves give voice to normally silent nocturnal paths as animals wander about, but unlike in snow, where their presence is preserved in foot-printed pathways, the leaves leave no lingering trace at all.

Awaiting winter

There is no defining day when winter starts, when the world in the Northern Hemisphere says "oh! now it is December, the meteorological start of winter. Now it is time to get cold" And yet in 2022 when I began writing this book, it seemed to have said just that, for going from an unusually warm autumn, we suddenly hit winter from the very beginning of the month.

The first week of that winter comprised a series of beautiful days with wonderful, magical nights. The days dreamy with thick frosts sparkling on all surfaces so that under the lamplight of dawn, the early morning seemed to shimmer in anticipation with the robin's bright notes serenading it into being. Amazing frost formations appeared on windscreens and bus shelters; each frond a fern accompanied by crystalline stars which sparkled like the cold twinkling of the real stars studding the winter sky. Mars was among them, the bringer of war, and I have always disliked Holst's orchestral piece of the same name. War is ever on the horizon, the battle drums beating on borders. One day the world will probably succumb, but then in that perfect present under the light of a full moon, all seemed sublime.

Technically it was still autumn, winter traditionally starting on December 21st, yet the frosty fields lingering in the deep blue glow of early morning seemed to shiver while the moonlight whispered "winter". It whispered through long, crystalline grasses and scribbled silver messages across the river's flowing course. The moonlight reflecting in the river reminded me of moonlit wading, when stark silver moonlight reflecting in the water, sparkled silver iridescence whenever I moved, dancing in delirious dreamy silver spirals about my feet. It was like bioluminescence in the sea; another wonder to blow the mind or transport it to dreamy reverie.

One particular morning in early December, a morning enhanced by hoar frost which hugged the trees and sparkled on the normally drab and mundane bracken fronds, transforming them into sculptures of symmetry with complex and beautiful form, I went to the water meadows. White wisps of mist were rising above a maze of textures and colours as I set up my camera, the sculpted structures of seedheads; every grass and reed encrusted in diamante, rough tall grass glazed thickly, softer riverside grasses swept with a dusting of ice. It was too much to take in, a feast for the eyes as the sunlight slanted through it in copper colours and pink-pearl tones, backlighting the frosted forms. With my camera, my fingers throbbing, I tried to capture this all too transient moment; a sight which is becoming increasingly rare as the world warms and our seasons become more non-descript.

Later, after a mug of chai latte, hands curled around cup, sitting outside one of the cafes in the December sunlight, I decided to further indulge my senses, for the vintage bookshop around the corner is a delight to every sense which I possess.

Stepping over the threshold of a Georgian house with its large fanlight and solid front door, I enter into a silent, serene interior which seems to gently and gracefully stand still. The smell of wood and polish, old books, and history (if one can indeed smell it!) greets me as much as a warm winking fire. The owner of the bookshop always willing to talk, friendly, engaging, welcomes me with a hot cup of tea.

Shelves filled with intrigue and interest, the words of people past, expert information, culture, history. It is an emporium which I cannot get enough of, and I could seriously stay here all day just browsing, watching time passing on the street outside beyond the window while I stay ensconced in timelessness. I would love to own a shop such as this.

Not knowing where to start that December day, I excitedly scanned the shelves. Children's books from the 50s when days seemed endless and carefree, and children created wild adventures without any adults. There was a freedom from danger, from the fear of being kidnapped, caught or killed as there is today, for roads are dangerous, cars fast and people are not all to be trusted. My mother always told me not to talk to strangers. That was a generation ago. When she was a child, it was less impersonal because everyone knew each other, there were communities. I grew up in this town and yet I no longer know many here.

I bought a book. A book about village life in the 1940s. A dream, a delight to read cuddled under a blanket on the sofa back home, being transported back in time to an Essex village of thatched cottages and a landscape shrouded in thick snow. In this book I meet a community with traditions, with joyful, carefree children skating on the river and exploring nature and where each adult is an individual; perhaps considered unremarkable today, but nevertheless a distinct character. The writer bemoans modernisation- the motor car, the fact that the village children went to school in the town, the loss of life as he knew it when he was young. The war changed so much even then, especially advancing technology. How much has it changed since? From my perspective, although the writer bemoans change, I am briefly taken back in time to something sweetly nostalgic, the whole book a winter-scape, snuggled under a blanket of snow where people live their lives in simple contentment. The snow then melts and there is the relief, the promise of spring, yet a spring mixed with dread. For while the winter was there and they were a community cut off, covered with snow, nothing could happen to them, and yet with the melt came the unknown, something new, the facing of fears, the war...

To the thrush, snuggled in her nest in the hedgerow, oblivious of the changing state of mankind, there was no fear. Her world had never changed since the dawn of time, as long as she could nest and feed and breed. Her only worry was the rearing of her chicks, she was perhaps in the 1940s unaffected by pesticides and global warming. But technology brings change and with it uncertainty. It happened with the Luddites, it happens today, and it happened with the war. For those stepping out of the snow, the thaw suggested new horrors, a war fought perhaps in a different way from those previously.

I see parallels with the pandemic of five years ago. Although not everyone experienced the same, for me personally, apart from horribly and desperately missing my family and friends who I couldn't see, it was a time when we were cocooned, shut off from the outside world and everything felt relatively safe and secluded like the thrush in the nest and the village under snow. Life seemed to stand still and with it, problems were put on hold. We became a community in our street, coming together to help one another out, to speak to one another from a distance. And yet there was imminent change, the way we used technology and had to adapt, meant we would never go back. There was also the knowledge of something out there beyond our four walls. Of those suffering, of those medical staff working hard while the pandemic continued, of those losing loved ones, of those dying. An old family friend died in the depths of pandemic; I deeply grieved his loss.

Cut off by the snow for a month or more,

the war in that 1940s Essex village seemed distant while people fought, people died, there was suffering on a scale which rocked the world and yet the community in the book were shut off from it for a while. And just as the thaw brought dread, a renewed reality, so the ease of pandemic restrictions brought more fears; a facing of new problems and a return of the old skeletons in the cupboard from which we had had respite.

My father grew up in the 1950s in an Essex village like the village in the book. He grew up on a small holding with chickens and ducks. There were orchards with apples, thick with blossom in spring and in the autumn full of fruit. There were plums too, sweet, sticky and ripe. These seem like idyllic carefree childhood days, but in reality, the scars of war would still be left as fresh and open wounds in many minds, minds which at the same time were breathing a sweet sense of thankfulness at being alive yet having to make sense of loss and change.

As we wrap up this book in winter, autumn teaches that change is inevitable, we cannot return to the past. It shows us that as time marches forward, things do change, life takes its course and while we focus on the present and the good times of the past, the future promises to repeat itself if we do not learn from past mistakes. It is therefore good to pick the apples while they are ripe, to look forward to the future and to make the most of autumn's rich bounty and of the good times. The bad times will always be knocking, waiting in the wings, but autumn teaches us how to be resourceful, to collect, store and save (not just the physical but by making memories), to care and provide for the people we love: our families and close friends. It emphasises the importance of these relationships, that we invest our time in them and appreciate them, ensuring that we are all sustained to survive the winter blows and stand against the inevitable thaw.

Acknowledgement:

A massive thank you to my great friends Ben and Julie for their input and support.

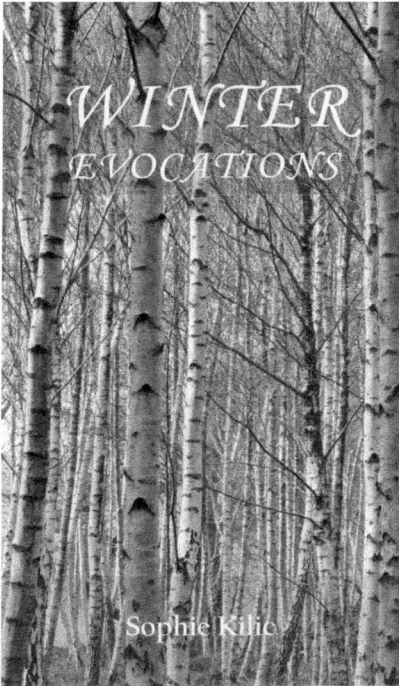

Winter Evocations is a celebration of winter. The long dark nights and colder days provide the perfect excuse to take a moment out, to put our feet up and indulge in a bit of comfort. This book is designed to dip into over a cosy hot drink, and perhaps make us feel better about this so often maligned season.

978-1-78222-823-3

https://www.amazon.co.uk/dp/B08VKT2WLK